Unbelievably
Good Deals and
Great Adventures
That You Absolutely
Can't Get Unless
You're a

DOG

Unbelievably Good Deals and Great Adventures That You Absolutely Can't Get Unless You're a

DOG

DARLENE ARDEN

McGraw·Hill

New York   Chicago   San Francisco   Lisbon   London   Madrid   Mexico City
Milan   New Delhi   San Juan   Seoul   Singapore   Sydney   Toronto

Library of Congress Cataloging-in-Publication Data

Arden, Darlene.
    Unbelievably good deals and great adventures that you absolutely can't get unless
you're a dog / Darlene Arden.
        p.   cm.
    ISBN 0-07-142103-3
    1. Dogs—Equipment and supplies.   2. Dog industry—United States—Directories.
I. Title.

SF427.15.A73   2004
636.7'0029'73—dc22   2004008085

1 2 3 4 5 6 7 8 9 0   DOC/DOC   3 2 1 0 9 8 7 6 5 4

ISBN 0-07-142103-3

McGraw-Hill books are available at special quantity discounts to use as premiums and
sales promotions, or for use in corporate training programs. For more information, please
write to the Director of Special Sales, Professional Publishing, McGraw-Hill, Two Penn
Plaza, New York, NY 10121-2298. Or contact your local bookstore.

For everyone who understands the joys of the human-animal bond.
And for my "chosen family." You know who you are.

Contents

Preface

Even a dyed-in-the-wool dog person like me can find new places to go, things to see, and stuff to buy. To be perfectly candid, I hate to shop unless it's for something animal related. In that case, I become a shopaholic. I've often told friends that if they're looking for me at a dog show, just follow the smell of melting plastic. And sightseeing is always more interesting when animals are involved. Raise your hand if you've taken pains to pick out the dogs and cats in various paintings while touring a museum.

If you're a dog owner, you're the target of big business because you are responsible for buying millions of dollars of dog-related products. More and more goods continue to appear in the marketplace trying to appeal to pet owners. The travel industry has seen the benefit of catering to pet owners as well. People who prefer to travel with their canine companions now have a much broader choice of hotels, motels, and amenities. As long as you act responsibly as an owner and keep the room clean and unharmed, dog owners will continue to be welcomed and will enjoy their dogs' company on trips. You can take dog-show tours with or without your dog. And, let's not forget all the items for people and their homes that have a dog motif. If you can imagine something dog related, it probably exists.

A former first lady of the United States said, "It takes a village to raise a child." It doesn't take a village to write a book, especially one like this, but it certainly helps if you have friends around the world who are willing to share their special places, ideas, gifts, and so forth to make life more fun with—and for—dogs. Those who should be singled out for special thanks are Deirdre Ashdown; Vanessa Amey; Sally Bahner; Donna Ball; Stuart Band; Tracie Barber; Lilian Barber; Louisa Beal, D.V.M.; Steve Dale; Debra Eldredge, D.V.M; Kate Fulkerson; Lary Lindsay; Drucilla Milligan; Jerri-Lynn Morrison; Shirley Moskow; Jennifer Ng; Suzanne Pirrie; Laurel Rabschutz; Lynne Rutenberg; Cheryl S. Smith; Jenette Smith; Jim Thurber; and Carol Whitney.

Discovering some of the many places to go, sights to see, and products to buy has been a lot of fun. And for the pleasure of this canine adventure I want to thank my editor Michele Pezzuti. And another thank-you to my literary agent, Meredith Bernstein, who takes care of business so I can enjoy my work.

When you find special dog-related treasures, share them with your dog-loving friends. It makes life so much more fun.

DISCLAIMER

Although I have done everything possible to ensure that the information in this book is as accurate as possible, there are bound to be listings that will be outdated by the time it reaches your hands. Unfortunately, some companies might not have survived in this competitive market and others may change their business practices.

Please be advised that the publisher cannot be held responsible for problems that you might encounter with any of these businesses. Please do not contact the publisher of this book about unfilled or improperly filled orders.

In fairness to our readers, we have not received payment from any of the companies so they could be listed in this book or could receive a better placement in this book. All companies have been treated equally and are simply listed in alphabetical order for your convenience.

1

Shop 'til You Drop

Shopping can be a magical experience if you have a goal in mind. Dog owners are happy to shop for virtually anything that features a canine image. Owners of purebred dogs are particularly happy to find something illustrating their specific breed. Some are so particular, that they insist that it be an exceptionally good representative of the breed.

There seems to be no limit as to where you can find dog-related merchandise. From stores to museum gift shops, to vendors at dog shows, to the Internet, the choices are dazzling—and a bit dizzying.

Here are some shopping options.

AJOLIE YARN MOTIFS

Accessories aren't just for people anymore; your dog can have them too. Ajolie Yarn Motifs creates fashion accessories for you and your furry companions. Of particular note is the scarf for dogs. The design is created to allow the collar to slip through the scarf so it stays in place. The scarves are available in a variety of designer novelty yarns in various colors and textures, along with other apparel. Owners can have a matching scarf made for their own fashion-forward look. These gems are part of a growing line of hand-knit, designer-look offerings from Ajolie Yarn Motifs, so check out the website periodically for new additions to the line as well as for any appearances at craft fairs.

For information: ajolieyarnmotifs.com; e-mail: ajolieyarnmotifs@aol .com; telephone and fax: 972-579-0565.

ALLFORPAWS

Allforpaws, a pet-bed company, was created by a woman with four handicapped Pomeranians. She wanted to make them feel comfortable, as they didn't like any of the pet beds she had purchased. They preferred her bed, which then inspired her to create a line of designer pet beds. Her dogs adored them.

The beds each have a picture frame that rests on the headboard and the designer look of the beds suits any room. The design raises the bed slightly off the floor, with open sides and front for easy access by your dog, making it accessible even for most pets who have medical conditions. The duvet has an envelope enclosure for easy removal and is machine washable. The beds offer affordable luxury. Each bed is 22" by 32" and comes in three styles. The Country Design has a rectangular base, ball feet, and a pitched headboard. It has bone shutters on each side of the picture frame to complement the design. It is tan with a coordinating duvet. The Neo-Classic design has square feet and an arched headboard separated by two columns. The base and column are off-white, and the headboard is sage green. The Modern style has a base with ball feet, an arched headboard, and a duvet that will complement any modern or contemporary setting. It has a neutral base color and a coordinating duvet.

For information: http://allforpaws.com; e-mail: jmirabito_allforpaws 5_8@msn.com; telephone: 603-882-1095; Allforpaws, P.O. Box 566, Nashua, NH 03061.

ANIMANIA

Animania is housed in the Westwood Animal Hospital complex, which is owned by veterinary behaviorist Dr. Wayne Hunthausen. Animania is owned by his wife, Jan Kyle, an interior designer. She carries a wide range of gifts for dogs and their owners, including handmade ceramics, stuffed toys, jewelry, picture frames, and framed art. Items for canines include bowls, beds, collars and leashes, carriers, treat jars, and toys.

A large Rousseau mural adorns Animania's back wall, near a stage used for speakers, classes, and special events. Events include a bite-prevention presentation for children, animal-themed art shows to benefit local shelters, pet Halloween and birthday parties, and the receptionist's annual Corgi party. Animania also offers ongoing obedience classes.

On one occasion, a Oaxacan carver demonstrated his skills by spending a week in the store creating animals out of wood. A photographer and writer who lived with the wood carvers in Mexico for several years accompanied him and presented a slide lecture.

The front of the store is the retail area and it has large skylights and a faux cloud ceiling, and faux palm trees support the sides. Special events and a sampling of products can be seen at their website; click on "Retail." Aside from the website, they also notify clientele about special events via their mailing list and news releases.

For information: westwoodanimalhospital.com; telephone: 913-362-2512; fax: 913-677-0203; Westwood Animal Hospital, 4820 Rainbow Blvd., Westwood, KS 66205.

ANYTHING ANIMALS

The online retailer Anything Animals has unusual animal-related merchandise. Their items for dogs are wonderfully practical and yet whimsical. You'll find matching bowls and mats; collars and leashes; and some really nifty furniture for dogs including beds that come shaped like a train, truck, drum, coffee cup, house, clock, fancy basket, human bed, or even one shaped like a trash can. Each is a conversation piece for humans while serving as a comfy bed for the dog. You can choose the color of the bed to coordinate with your home decor.

Anything Animals also carries grooming items, pillows, and treats. If you visit their website, you'll see an international currency shopping converter at the bottom of every page. They accept phone or fax orders, and you can print out an order form from their website if you prefer to mail in your order. Orders are shipped within twenty-four to forty-eight hours.

For information: anythinganimals.com; e-mail: customerservice@ anythinganimals.com; telephone: 321-953-8184; fax: 321-953-8184; corporate address: Anything Animals, 1153 Malabar Rd., Suite 8-160, Palm Bay, FL 32907.

THE BACK YARD

This company specializes in "special gifts for special people." Their emphasis is on dog-related collectibles. The owners, who have been involved in many dog sports over the years, have created their own dog items and commissioned others. The Back Yard has everything from rubber stamps to T-shirts to note cards. All dog collectibles are listed by breed; click on your favorite breed to determine which items are available.

The Back Yard also features Rug Dog Designs in a variety of breeds and items. Each illustrated breed shows the dog at rest but ready to join you for playtime at any moment. Rug Dog Designs are available on decals, hats, mats, sweatshirts, tote bags, and, of course, T-shirts. They also carry some dog supplies including a sunshade for your dog to block out UV rays.

For information: the-back-yard.com; e-mail: thebackyard@starband .net; telephone (toll-free): 877-707-K9K9 or (local): 810-724-8615.

BARKER & MEOWSKY

Chicago is home to the "paw" firm of Barker & Meowsky. They carry a wide range of items for dogs and cats as well as for their humans and home. Looking for a hula outfit for your dog? A cowboy hat? How about a sterling silver or a pewter ID tag? Barker & Meowsky have fancy carrier bags and even fancier beds. They offer remarkable-looking bowls that resemble modern art; leash packs; grooming items; and holiday items, including a talking Christmas tree toy. You can find treats at Barker & Meowsky along with decorative items for the home, including decoupage frames, hand-painted plaques, needlepoint pillows, and more.

You can join their mailing list to keep up to date with what's happening at Barker & Meowsky. They have a very reasonable return and exchange policy. (You can find details on their website.)

If you stop by their store, your four-legged friend will receive a yummy treat. Barker & Meowsky host a variety of events for pets and people. You can check for those at their website or when you visit the store.

For information: barkerandmeowsky.com; e-mail: orders@barkerand meowsky.com; telephone: 773-868-0200; fax: 773-868-0222; Barker & Meowsky, 1003 W. Armitage, Chicago, IL 60614 or Barker & Meowsky, 3319 N. Broadway, Chicago, IL 60657.

BEASTLY FURNISHINGS

While retailers do carry their products, you can order directly from Beastly Furnishings via phone, fax, or e-mail. They will also custom make some products, including sofas and beds, using your fabric to match your furniture. If you prefer sleeping bags, chaises, pillows, sofas, or day beds, you'll find an assortment of interesting dog furniture here. Mitered corners, rolled arms—all the styling you expect in your own furniture. Synthetic downlike fiber fills the pillows.

For information: beastlyfurnishings.com; e-mail: sales@beastly furnishings.com; telephone: 402-392-1976; fax: 402-398-3054.

CHERRYBROOK

If you've attended a dog show in the eastern part of the United States, it's very likely that you have encountered Cherrybook. They're easy to spot with their blue- and white-striped awning and plethora of dog supplies that include grooming equipment and products, show leads, bedding, books, bowls, crates, exercise pens, and more. You can also find dog-breed watches, dog toys, and sweaters and coats. They also do a brisk mail-order business. And if you happen to find yourself passing through Broadway, New Jersey, you can visit their retail store, grab a shopping cart, and pick up supplies and toys for your canine (or feline) companion. Cherrybrook bills itself as "The Ultimate in Dog and Cat Supplies," and you'll find an amazing array of categories listed in their online menu.

For information: cherrybrook.com; e-mail: custserv@cherrybrook .com; telephone (toll-free): 800-524-0820 or (local): 908-689-7979; fax: 908-689-7988; Cherrybrook, Inc., Box 15, Route 57 (or 2257 Route 57 is the street address if you're planning to visit), Broadway, NJ 08808. (Store hours are Monday through Saturday, 9 A.M. to 7 P.M., and Sunday, 9 A.M. to 5 P.M., EST.)

CLINGY CANINES

Obviously, Clingy Canines gets its name from one of the products they sell: window clings, which are simply peel and stick—no adhesive and no mess. This online retailer offers clings that have the look of stained-glass sun-catchers at a fraction of the cost. They will adhere to any smooth surface: car or house windows, your front door, or even one of your kitchen appliances. The possibilities are only limited by your imagination.

A special paint that dries to a semitransparent, plastic-like substance is used so that light shines through the window cling. When dry, the paint retains some of its tacky qualities, which help it to adhere to almost any smooth surface. The clings can be moved and repositioned. Although they will stick to painted walls or wood, this is not recommended as they sometimes remove the paint or varnish from these surfaces.

Clingy Canines has an entire section of window clings, featuring more than 183 different breeds. Most are illustrated in different poses so you can choose the one you prefer. When you access their website, click on the breed that interests you, and the variety of products and poses in which it's available will appear.

Along with window clings, Clingy Canines also has ornaments, each one handmade so no two will be exactly alike.

Clingy Canines specializes in creating full custom clings from your favorite photo or your kennel logo, even if it's an animal that they don't normally do. They can make either a cling or ornament from the photo you provide. Check their website for pricing on products and custom orders.

To get an exact price quote on a custom order, e-mail a picture to them and include the dimensions you want as well as the quantity. You can see samples of their custom work on their website and you can sign up for their sale and promotional newsletter.

For information: clingycanines.com; e-mail: clingycanines@aol.com; telephone and fax: 716-894-7210; Clingy Canines, 2687 Harlem Rd., Cheektowaga, NY 14225.

COSETTE'S CLOSET

This Internet business, based in Southern California, gets its name from the site owner's less-than-two-pound Yorkshire Terrier service dog, Cosette.

Among the products featured are Cosette's Choice healthy biscuits in a wide range of flavors. Cosette's Closet also offers a wide range of products for small dogs, including a line of original clothing, although goods can be special ordered for larger dogs. You'll also find delightful items for the home, notepaper, safe car seats, books, carriers, jewelry for people and pets, and some rather unusual items including your dog's very own "Park Place," which features a small patch of grass with its own irrigation system. You can also purchase sofas, unusual beds, even a doggie armoire. The list goes on and on. Cosette's Private Collection is a range of natural bath and beauty products for your dog. A natural household cleaner is also available.

For information: cosettescloset.com and cosettesprivatecollection.com; e-mail: deb@cosettescloset.com; telephone (toll-free): 877-267-3883 or (local): 949-218-0277.

DIADEC DOGS

The online retailer Diadec Dogs offers canine collectibles and features the work of Chainsaw Canines, by Dennis Sullivan and Frances Conklin, as well as The Pleet Collection, which is the work of Lynda Pleet. These distinctive designs of dog collectibles are created in different mediums.

Chainsaw Canines are quite literally individually carved by chainsaw from ponderosa pine, and they're hand painted. Each Chainsaw Dog sports a red bandanna and has its own "license" tucked under the bandanna or beneath the body. The ponderosa pine used is an environmentally friendly product since they don't harvest live trees to create their canine sculptures. Instead, they use trees that have succumbed to the natural process of disease, lightning, or wind damage. Chainsaw Canines have been on display at the AKC Museum of the Dog, the Lewis & Clark Bicentennial Celebration, and featured on QVC (television shopping channel). The carvings come in two sizes: a tabletop carving, about 9 inches tall, and a patio guard, approximately 14″ by 18″ tall. The Chainsaw Canines come in more than forty breeds. If you don't see your breed on the website, you're invited to ask about it. Because of the creative process, it usually takes three weeks for the Chainsaw Canines to be delivered. The Patio Guards take six to eight weeks because of the availability of wood and the drying time. Certain breeds can be custom painted.

The Pleet Collection is more contemporary than Chainsaw Canines. Lynda Pleet creates her dogs from solid-cast, porcelain resin, and then she hand paints, dates, and signs them. Custom finishes are available. Each is approximately 6″ by 4″, or you could purchase larger ones that are approximately 12 inches in height. The Pleet Collection is available in about twenty-five different breeds. Lynda Pleet also creates cat collectibles.

Diadec Dogs has a volume discount and affiliate program for rescue and shelter groups.

For information: chainsawcanine.com; e-mail: info@diadecdogs.com; Diadec Designs, 258 Legate Hill Rd., Leominster, MA 01453.

THE DOG BAR

The Dog Bar is a full-service, luxury pet-supply store in Miami Beach's Lincoln Road shopping district. They cater to dogs and cats and their humans. The store covers two thousand square feet and mixes vintage collectibles with handmade fixtures reflecting all things canine. They are open seven days a week until late night. Their online store allows people to shop from home, wherever home might be.

The Dog Bar offers everything from custom collars and leashes to unique toys, gift items, shampoos, conditioners, sweaters, harnesses, and much, much more. And, their products are cruelty free. They offer a 100 percent, total satisfaction guarantee. If you're not satisfied with your merchandise—and it's unused with packaging intact—it may be returned for a full refund or online credit within thirty days of purchase. Details are on the website. You can order online, via telephone, or by mail.

The Dog Bar also showcases local and national artists who feature animals in their work. Often, they display their art in the store. You can contact the store for information to purchase or commission artwork; artwork samples are available on the website.

The Dog Bar is concerned with the community and hosts adoption events in the store. And they also offer doggie birthday parties in their bar, featuring a homemade birthday cake for dogs.

For information: dogbar.com; e-mail: customerservice@dogbar.com; telephone (toll-free): 866-4-DOGBAR or (local): 305-532-5654 (Phone orders are taken seven days a week, 10 A.M. to 10 P.M.); fax: 305-672-9921; The Dog Bar, Inc., 723 N. Lincoln Ln., Miami Beach, FL 33139-2903.

DOG COLLECTIBLES

This online business offers a variety of collectible items in a growing selection of dog breeds. Their products include dog jewelry, hand-crafted sculptures, figurines, art, note cards, Christmas tree ornaments, and more. The pieces are created by artisans who come from around the world.

Because the owner travels to dog shows around the world, he looks for specific breed items upon request, with the understanding that these items will take longer to locate and ship. Dog Collectibles carries a number of rare breed items and will be adding more as they become available.

The website is easy to navigate and the home page includes alphabetized links to lists of dog breeds. Each link contains the products that are available in that particular breed. Dog Collectibles accepts credit cards, personal checks, bank checks, or money orders.

For information: dogcollectibles.com; e-mail: info@dogcollectibles
.com; telephone: 978-443-8387; fax: 978-443-0183; Dog Collectibles,
P.O. Box 377, Sudbury, MA 01776.

DOGS LIFE TRAVEL PRODUCTS & INFORMATION

This website has products for the dog who is on the go, including a
Pup-Tent™ Travel Crate; kennel and crate pads; and a clever Rollover®
Travel Pack and Bed for dogs that carries dog food, water, a bowl, and
other items your dog will need. It opens to an indoor-outdoor dog
bed. The company specializes in custom-size products. All of their
products are handmade in the United States. You'll also find winter
fleece scarves and caps for dog owners, as well as information links.
They warn that you must be a dog lover to enter their website. They
will only accept credit card orders by phone.

For information: dogs-life.com; e-mail: info@dogs-life.com; telephone:
541-547-3464; Dogs Life, Inc., P.O. Box 652, Newport, OR 97365.

ESPECIALLY FOR PETS

This small chain of half a dozen stores in Massachusetts serves as a
reference for those who want information as well as supplies, lectures,
and classes in obedience and agility. The stores were created by pet
lovers for pet lovers. They also feature grooming and nail clipping,
which is done for a five-dollar donation that goes to a local pet charity, newly chosen each month.

Not only can you buy basic supplies, but they're not going to sell
you something you don't need. For example, if you have a puppy and
want a pet bed, they're going to explain why a crate would be better
for a pup who is not yet housetrained.

Most of these stores have regularly scheduled cat adoption days in
association with the Massachusetts SPCA. Classes offered at their stores
include puppy kindergarten, canine good citizen, Reiki, TTouch,
second-chances classes for rescue dogs, and troubleshooting classes
for specific problems; seminars include nutrition and new puppy care.

Their website lists upcoming seminars, news, and so forth, and
they have an e-mail club that includes a monthly newsletter and per-

sonalized birthday card and gift for your pet. And there's a local pet photographer who regularly goes to the store to take photos of pets by appointment. The exception is the Wayland Store, where they only do Christmas photos with Santa.

For information: especiallyforpets.com.

FEATHERED GEMS JEWELRY

This Internet company has some wonderful sterling silver and gem-stone items, and the owner donates a portion of the purchase price to various Greyhound rescue groups. Dog charms, which can be used to create earrings, pendants, and pins, are available in a variety of breeds. Questions about their designs, special orders, beadwork, and so forth can be sent to Feathered Gems (address follows), or you can e-mail from the website. Contact Kathy Johnson to request a product list and prices.

For information: featheredgems.com; telephone (answering machine) and fax: 313-928-9123; Feathered Gems Jewelry, P.O. Box 722, Lincoln Park, MI 48146.

GERONIMO'S™, LTD., OF NANTUCKET

This store—named after the late dog of owner Jan Jaeger—offers every-thing from pet food to toys, to beds, bowls, and doggie diners. You can also find nautical-themed leather collars and gifts for your dog with a Nantucket theme, such as a dog biscuit in the shape of the island. For the dog owner, you can find tote bags, aprons, board games, books, cal-endars, and much, much more.

The store is well laid out and delightful. Geronimo's always has a cat from the MSPCA shelter who is available for adoption, a nice way to help the pet community of Nantucket.

Shopping online is a treat. Not only is the site easy to navigate, but the owner is the local newspaper's pet columnist, and her columns are posted on Geronimo's website. If you are looking for art-metal garden sculptures, stained-glass sun-catchers, or a kit to make a paw-print keepsake, you'll find it at Geronimo's. You can also purchase hand-painted, hanging dog ornaments. The Brant Point Lighthouse ornaments (available online or in the store) each depicts a dog (available in a variety of breeds) in front of the lighthouse.

For information: geronimos.com; e-mail: mailorders@geronimos.com; telephone (toll-free: 800-738-7297 or (local): 508-228-3731; Geronimo's, Ltd., of Nantucket, 119 Pleasant St., Nantucket, MA 02554.

THE GLITZY LADY

The Glitzy Lady can be found at many dog shows in the Northeast and on the Internet. The owner, Sharon Brown, carries unique handcrafted animal jewelry and gifts and her items include some interesting creations. Brown buys stones at gem and mineral shows and creates boxes and pins with dogs on the gems. She has an interesting array of dog-breed pins, some made from real postage stamps, and others are original creations from several artists whose work she carries. She also has some interesting dog-breed plates, rhinestone pins, and some sculpture that is whimsical and fun.

For information: theglitzylady.com; e-mail: glitzy100@aol.com; telephone: 203-924-5663; Sharon Brown, 255 Kneen St. #20, Shelton, CT 06484.

IN THE COMPANY OF DOGS

This upscale catalog retailer also has an online presence. They have a wonderful array of merchandise for dogs and their people, including a humorous doggie whirligig that looks like modern art; dog beds; an ID tag that comes with a twenty-four-hour recovery service; treats; and clothing for dogs and their human companions. You can also find sculpture; fancy collars and leashes; handbags; key rings; magnets; and jewelry, including sterling silver breed charms.

They also offer a paw-proof screen for your door; a doggie ramp; car seats; doormats; figurines; note cards; sculpture tables; toys for dogs and humans; stairs for your dog to use to access furniture; collectors' items; and more.

For information: inthecompanyofdogs.com; telephone (toll-free): 800-544-4595 (Phone is available twenty-four hours a day.); fax (toll-free): 800-952-5638; In the Company of Dogs, P.O. Box 3330, Chelmsford, MA 01824-0930.

JB WHOLESALE PET SUPPLIES

JB Wholesale has both a paper catalog and a website. Owned by dog fanciers (one has bred more than 188 AKC champions and more than 300 champions worldwide), they understand the needs of dog owners, breeders, groomers, and people who show their dogs. They carry more than five thousand items for dogs and cats and they offer only premium brands of food. You can find everything from beds, collars, and leashes, to grooming supplies; clothing; supplements; products for dental, ear, and eye care; ex-pens; toys; and much more.

The website features a library with articles on topics such as the importance of crate training, and you can also find a glossary of nutritional terms. It also spotlights close-out as well as new items.

They stand behind everything they sell with a thirty-day, money-back guarantee; they will either issue a refund, credit, or exchange the item. They have three different outlet store locations in New Jersey where you can shop.

For information: jbpet.com; e-mail: customerservice@jbpet.com; telephone (toll-free United States and Canada): 800-526-0388 or (local): 201-405-1111 (Telephone orders can be taken Monday through Friday, 8:30 A.M. to 10:00 P.M.; Saturdays, 9:30 A.M. to 4:30 P.M.; and Sundays, 11 A.M. to 4 P.M. EST.); fax (toll-free): 800-788-5005 or (local): 201-405-1706; JB Wholesale Pet Supplies, 5 Raritan Rd., Oakland, NJ 07436. *Outlet store locations:* 347 Ramapo Valley Rd., Oakland, NJ, telephone: 201-405-0042. (Store hours are Monday through Friday, 9 A.M. to 8 P.M.; Saturday, 9 A.M. to 6 P.M.; and Sunday, 11 A.M. to 4 P.M.) 289 Wagaraw Rd., Hawthorne, NJ, telephone: 973-423-9333. (Store hours are Monday through Friday, 9 A.M. to 8 P.M.; Saturday, 9 A.M. to 6 P.M.; and Sunday, 11 A.M. to 4 P.M.) 500 South River St., Riverfront Shopping Plaza, Hackensack, NJ, telephone: 201-931-0247. (Store hours are Monday through Friday, 9 A.M. to 8 P.M.; Saturday, 9 A.M. to 6 P.M.; and Sunday, 11 A.M. to 4 P.M.)

JUSTDOGPOOP.COM

This online company specializes in unique dog collars, leashes, and pet beds. Collars and leashes are made from handmade leather and crystals; others are adorned with faux fur and flowers. Your dog is sure to be noticed on that daily walk sporting one of these creations. The designer bowls are really worth looking at; from jester bowls to a coliseum bowl, and more; these aren't just dog dishes—they're conversation pieces and will certainly add something to your home decor. The dog beds are snuggly warm, as are the cozy coats. They also carry an assortment of toys for your companion. They shop worldwide so a visit to their website will provide an assortment of items from a variety of locales.

For information: justdogpoop.com; e-mail (questions): info@justdog poop.com or store@justdogpoop.com; telephone: 610-983-9595; fax: 610-983-3395; JustDogPoop, P.O. Box 305, Phoenixville, PA 19460.

KLUTZILUV

Klutzy was the owner's first champion West Highland White Terrier, and the company name is an ongoing tribute to the dog. This website features upscale items for dogs and owners. Occasionally, you'll find a Klutziluv booth at a dog show on the east coast where they display high-quality merchandise.

Klutziluv features everything from jewelry, handbags, sweaters, slippers, collectibles, and art prints, to items for the dog including collars and leads. The hand-painted items are exclusive to Klutziluv. They also sell some items on eBay.

For information: klutziluv.net; e-mail: klutziluv@aol.com; telephone: 718-506-8759.

KURANDA DOG BEDS

These chew-proof beds are ideal for any home. Their clean lines blend with any décor, and they're both healthy and supportive for the dog. The fabric is tucked inside a PVC frame. The bed is both lightweight and noncorrosive, which means that you can also place one outside so your dog can relax on the patio or by the pool. The bed comes in several sizes, and you have a choice of fabrics. They also come in a choice of poly resin or metal. The company also sells the fabric separately, so you can change colors or replace worn fabric at any time, which is a nice feature. The company makes the beds available at a special price to rescue groups.

For information: kuranda.com; telephone (toll-free): 800-752-5308; fax: 410-266-3944; Kuranda USA, P.O. Box 6651, Annapolis, MD 21401.

MUTTROPOLIS

Muttropolis has an online presence and two stores that you can visit in Southern California. They feature an assortment of designer beds, pet bowls, toys, clothing for your canine friend, freshly baked treats made with human-grade ingredients, gift items, and more with lots of things for your dog, your cat, and you.

Your dog is not only welcome in the stores, but they also have "pooch parties" so you can celebrate your canine friend's birthday or other special occasions. They even have a lounge, furnished with pet couches, so your friend can come and sit and enjoy movies that are geared to dogs. The stores also hold animal-adoption events. They are very much aware of the need to find homes for homeless pets.

For information: muttropolis.com; e-mail: bark@muttropolis.com; telephone: 858-755-DOGS; fax: 858-755-3648. *Store locations:* 227 South Cedros, Solana Beach, CA 92075 and 7755 Girard Ave., La Jolla, CA 92037.

OLD TOWN PET PALACE

With shops in Kissimmee, Florida, and Myrtle Beach, South Carolina, as well as an online business, Old Town Pet Palace provides fun shopping for the pet owner. Their merchandise includes everything from stoneware sculpture to dog angels, which can either be placed on display or hung from a Christmas tree. They have items in specific breeds, and while they can't always find something readily available in your breed, they can custom design items such as leashes, T-shirts, ID tags, and more. The links page on their website is growing and includes at least one dog rescue group.

For information: petpalace.com; e-mail: e-mail@petpalace.com; telephone: 407-297-9215; fax (you can print out their order form): 407-297-9125. *Store locations:* Broadway at the Beach, Myrtle Beach, SC, telephone: 843-444-2744. Old Town Shopping Attraction, Kissimmee, FL, telephone: 407-396-7260.

PAWZESSIONS

PawZessions specializes in personalized pet products, especially customized pet bowls and treat jars in a range of designs and colors. All personalized items are hand painted to order. They also personalize humorous signs and distressed picture frames, and they continue to add to their growing list of products from which you can choose. A sampling of available designs can be found on their website, such as wooden place signs and hand-painted, dishwasher-safe ceramic bowls in a choice of sizes; you can choose from round or fluted styles. You will also find fire hydrant or round treat jars, their exclusive "Dotty Collection" of pet dinnerware, and their Nazdog Collections for NASCAR fans.

PawZessions ships internationally. President George W. Bush and Laura Bush are among the well known whose pets have personalized items from PawZessions because they provided the White House with personalized bowls for the current four-legged occupants.

Visit their store where they have a dog "barkery" section featuring home-baked dog treats with no preservatives or harmful ingredients. The barkery looks like a *boulangerie* in Paris and even has a canopy. They also feature a menu of the week. Dogs are, of course, welcome at the store; the owners enjoy having canine customers visit.

For information: pawzessions.com; e-mail: pawzessions@aol.com; telephone and fax: 805-374-1979, PawZessions, 3110 W. Adirondack Ct., Westlake Village, CA 91362. *Store location:* PawZessions Pet Boutique & Bakery, 2989 E. Thousand Oaks Blvd., Thousand Oaks, CA 91362, telephone and fax: 805-449-1022.

PUPPS PROFLEECE

What's so special about fleece that's imported from England? ProFleece is a nifty bedding for your dog that's comfortable, durable, practically chew-proof, and will last for years. This easy-to-care-for fleece looks thick and heavy but it's made of polyester so it's machine washable, and you can tumble dry it at a very low heat. It will look fluffier if you air fluff or dry it on a clothesline instead of using a heated dryer. If you have a puppy, you will especially appreciate the fact that it gives him or her good footing and liquids pass through it leaving the surface dry if your little one has an accident. Another benefit of polyester is that it's nonallergenic and nontoxic and it is a nonirritant. It won't support bacterial growth, it resists permanent staining, and it's flame retardant. Used in veterinary practices, it's also useful for whelping, incontinence, and for sick or elderly dogs or cats as well as for the comfort of healthy dogs and cats. ProFleece is reasonably priced and comes in a range of sizes including those to fit most crates. You can also purchase it by the yard. Custom sizes are also available. Prices are subject to change so check with the company.

For information: http://fleecebedding.com; e-mail: orlane@fast.net; telephone: 302-659-1811.

PUTTIN' ON THE DOG

This mail-order business has both a print catalog and a website. At the present time, they can only fill orders from the United States and Canada. With a wide range of products, they have items with specific breed motifs, featuring everything from banners and jewelry to needlepoint pillows and art prints. They carry such a wide range of products that it would require too much space to list them all.

For information: puttinonthedog.com; telephone (toll-free): 800-720-8005 or (local): 770-498-1233 (Phone hours are Monday through Friday, 9 A.M. to 5 P.M., EST.); fax (anytime): 770-498-1750; Puttin' on the Dog, 1980-C Parker Ct., Stone Mountain, GA 30087.

RAINING CATS & DOGS

This South Carolina shop specializes in novelty items featuring—yes—cats and dogs! The merchandise includes T-shirts, mugs, books, calendars, magnets, cards, umbrellas, pictures, hats, collars, bandannas, ornaments, and plaques. You can find Raining Cats & Dogs in the Carousel Courtyard at Barefoot Landing.

For information: telephone (toll-free): 800-272-2320 or (local): 843-272-8349; Raining Cats & Dogs, Barefoot Landing, 4898 Hwy. 17, North Myrtle Beach, SC 29582.

SHERBERT STUFF

SherBert Stuff can be found at dog shows around the country or on the Internet. Some boutiques around the United States are also carrying them, so keep your eyes open! They have an interesting line of products, all designed to keep your dogs cool in hot weather and warm in the cold. The products are filled with special little crystals and directions for use, and care instructions come with each item. Their products include cool mats, cool coats, cool neck rolls, cool raincoats, cool pouches, and squish beds. All of the products are handcrafted in Pennsylvania's Pocono Mountains.

For information: sherbertstuff.com; e-mail: info@sherbertstuff.com; telephone: 570-688-4084; fax: 570-688-1125; SherBert Stuff, RR6, Box 6480B, Saylorsburg, PA 18353.

THE SIGN BARN

While they do visit various dog shows in the East, you don't have to leave your home to shop at The Sign Barn. If you want to display your dog's breed on your car, mailbox, or in other prominent places, this online retailer is for you. They carry decals for your vehicle or mailbox, including some with your dog's breed made from an American flag design. They have magnetic signs, banners, vinyl lettering, PVC and vinyl signs, carved signs, animal cutouts, and hardware packages. What's more, they have virtually every breed available including Affenpinscher and Brussels Griffon, which aren't exactly common.

For information: signbarn.com; e-mail: signbarn@bcn.net; telephone: 413-229-2292; fax: 413-229-2274; The Sign Barn, 247 S. Undermountain Rd., Sheffield, MA 01257.

SITSTAY.COM

This website-only business, based in Lincoln, Nebraska, has a plethora of items for the dog owner. They are also one of DogRead (an online seminar reading group) list's vendors for the online book seminars. Along with books, they sell clothing, edibles, equipment, toys, grooming supplies, supplements, vet wrap, gifts and cards, and more. They also have a dog comic page, message boards, a free monthly e-mail newsletter, and more. Amusingly, when you e-mail them from their website, an automated acknowledgment—"written" by the dogs at Sit-Stay—arrives before the response.

For information: sitstay.com; telephone (toll-free for orders): 800-SIT-STAY or (local for general information): 402-467-3426 (Phone hours are Monday through Friday, 8 A.M. through 5 P.M., CST.); fax: 402-467-5055; SitStay.com, 5831 N. 58th St., Suite 1, Lincoln, NE 68507.

TAILS BY THE LAKE

Tails by the Lake was opened in Sausalito in 1999, but you don't have to live in California to shop there. They have a fairly comprehensive website that allows you to shop at home. The owners' desire to find unique items for their own two dogs led them to create the store's concept and later the website. Their dogs, Utah (a Chesapeake Bay Retriever) and Leo (a Chow-Lab cross), are an integral part of the business who help choose snacks, toys, and accessories that will suit their friends. Tails by the Lake also has merchandise for felines and for the humans in the family. They even have a gift registry and gift certificates. Among the items available are paintings and original art, clocks, clothing, dog-breed items, comical doormats, leash hooks, wine bottle corks, dog and cat gift items, an umbrella for your dog, purses and handbags for the owner, books, and dog and cat jewelry.

You can return any item within thirty days of purchase for exchange or refund. However, special order items (breed items, artwork, doghouses, personalized merchandise, or any item that has a shipping time listed) cannot be returned. More details are at their website.

The owners realize that not all dogs and cats are as lucky as Utah and Leo, so they donate a portion of their profits to agencies that strive to help less fortunate animals. The website reminds visitors to spay and neuter their pets and suggests that if someone is looking for a purebred, he or she should check rescue groups first. You can visit their store at the base of Squaw Valley Ski Mountain at the Village at Squaw Valley, or you can call toll-free. You can also e-mail any questions you might have about your order.

For information: tailsbythelake.com; e-mail: info@tailsbythelake.com; telephone (toll-free): 877-464-3364 or (local or international): 530-

583-WAGS (Orders are taken Sunday through Friday, 10 A.M. to 6 P.M., PST.); Village at Squaw Valley, Olympic Valley, CA 96146.

INTERNATIONAL

AROMATHERAPY GOLD

Today's interest in aromatherapy even extends to pets. England's Aromatherapy Gold makes dog-collar tags with essential oils that are released once the tags are unwrapped. In theory, the dog—depending upon the individual tag—is uplifted, relaxed, revitalized, or protected against insects. The tags are available to order online and are reportedly safe, but owners are warned NOT to use them on dogs younger than one year of age, nor should children be allowed to play with the tags. They are for external use only, and you must wash your hands after putting the tag on the dog's collar. The four blends are flea/tick control; deodorant; pick me up/after illness, injury, or operation; and relaxing/calming.

For information: aromatherapygold.com; e-mail: info@aromatherapy gold.com; telephone: 01509 600433; fax: 01509 650501; Aromatherapy Gold, Highfields House, Belton, Loughborough, Leicestershire, United Kingdom, LE12 9XA.

AURORALITES SAFETY COLLAR

This safety collar keeps you and your dog safe when you go out walking after dark. This quality, lighted dog collar has been used by search-and-rescue professionals and dog handlers around the world and is now available to the general public. Other lighted collars are on the market, but this one is manufactured and assembled in North America using excellent components. The collars are reinforced, waterproofed, tested, and warranted. Reflective collars or vests don't work unless they're caught by headlights, but the Auroralites Safety Collar has a battery and lights up when the collar is turned on, so you can be seen only when you want to be. This collar doesn't strobe or flash but has a blue light that's more penetrating and can be seen more easily in inclement weather. You can see the collar online where you can also order. While some retailers might carry the Auroralites Safety Collar, you're better off visiting their website for detailed product and purchasing information.

For every twenty-five collars ordered, Auroralites will donate $100 to the designated rescue organization that is registered with them. Pricing on the website is in U.S. currency.

For information: auroralites.com; e-mail: auroralites@auroralites.com; telephone: 905-820-2980; Auroralites, 2231 Blue Beech Crescent, Mississauga, ON,.L5L 1C2, Canada.

BEANIES & BELVEDERE

Beanies & Belvedere Designs for Dogs calls themselves "fun, funky, and fabulous." Beanies and Belvedere are, of course, the dogs who belong to the company's owners, two designers in Burnaby, British Columbia. They have turned their talents to creating fashionable outerwear for dogs. Their canine clothing is available at a variety of stores in Canada. Some U.S. shops also carry their togs for dogs.

For information: beaniesandbelvedere.com; e-mail: info@beaniesand belvedere.com; telephone: 604-306-3630; fax: 604-540-8877.

BLACK DOG WEAR

Black Dog Wear is an Australian company that specializes in high-quality, canine training equipment, including custom-made items, such as a sling for a dog with balance problems. They have a commitment to positive training reinforcement methods and offer harnesses, including car harnesses; training accessories; and Black Dog logo clothing items for the owner. They back their products with a quality guarantee. You can order from their website or find their products at veterinary clinics, dog-training organizations, and selected pet supply stores in Australia.

For information: blackdog.net.au; e-mail: orders@blackdog.net.au; telephone: (03) 9762 4782; fax: (03) 9762 0885.

BRONZE IMPRESSIONS

Bronze baby shoes used to be quite popular. Then along came bronzed handprints. This company in England takes it a step further; they not only bronze children's handprints, but they will bronze your dog's paw print. Cast in solid bronze and mounted on a decorative plaque, this is an unusual keepsake of a beloved companion. The castings are hand poured, receiving individual attention, and subject to "rigorous" quality assurance.

Once confirmation of your order is received, the company will mail you a kit, which you use to take an imprint of your dog's paw. Once you're happy with the results of the imprints, you send the kit back to Bronze Impressions. In about two weeks, you will receive your bronze casting on a decorative wooden stand.

For information: bronzeimpressions.co.uk; e-mail: info@bronze impressions.co.uk; telephone: 0115 932 6446; Bronze Impressions, Freepost NEA15385, 111 Station Rd., Stanley Village, Derbyshire, DE7 6BF, United Kingdom.

FETCH—A DOG'S DOG STORE

Fetch—A Dog's Dog Store is located in Kerrisdale, in Vancouver, British Columbia. The area boasts of many well-cared-for dogs. Fetch is a dog experience, a specialized store for dogs and their owners. They have their own line of dog furniture, along with other doggie necessities, such as raincoats, accessories, and more. You can subscribe to their newsletter online, and you can print out a discount coupon found in the promotion section of their website.

For information: fetchstore.ca; e-mail: dogs@fetchstore.ca; telephone: 604-879-DOGS; fax: 604-879-3640; *Store location:* Fetch, 5617 West Blvd., Vancouver, BC, V6M 4W7, Canada. (Store hours are Monday through Friday, 10 A.M. to 7 P.M.; Saturday, 9:30 A.M. to 6 P.M.; and Sunday noon to 5 P.M.)

KIMBOS PET WEAR

This New Zealand company (they have a distributor in Australia for their products) carries a variety of items including "bitches britches" for female dogs in heat or incontinent canines, Cooltek coats, life jackets for dogs who go boating, saddlebags for doggie hikers, travel bowls that fold for easy transport, collars and leads, cooling mats, bandannas, and winter coats.

For information: kimbospetwear.com; e-mail: info@kimbospetwear
.com; telephone (toll-free in New Zealand): 0800-254626 or 64-9-
2697680; fax: 64-9-2697681; Kimbos Pet Wear, P.O. Box 75-651,
Manurewa, Auckland, New Zealand.

PAMPET DOG FASHIONS AND ACCESSORIES

Pampet carries a wide range of clothing and accessories for dogs and
cats. You'll find everything from holiday costumes to seasonal wear,
such as bikinis, raincoats, winter clothing, sports jerseys, carrier bags,
and much, much more. Based in Thailand and Singapore, the company retails locally and exports internationally. They have distributors
in the United Kingdom and the United States. You can find measuring
charts on the website so that you can properly measure your dog for
the type of clothing you're purchasing. Pampet USA distributes all over
the United States and the Americas.

Petlondon, Ltd., in the United Kingdom stocks and supplies several of their collections including beds, shoes, and pants.

For information: pampetusa.com (or pampet.com will take you to
their main website); e-mail: info@pampetusa.com or (United Kingdom): pampet@petlondon.com; telephone: 866-4 PAMPET or (outside
of the United States): 949-645-2204 or (Petlondon, U.K.): +44 (0)
800 083 3418; fax: 949-645-1080.

PASSION FOR DOGS

Passion for Dogs specializes in twenty-four-carat, gold-plated lace dog
jewelry as well as cat jewelry. More than seventy-eight breeds—from
Afghan Hound to Yorkshire Terrier—and six styles are available, with
more being added. A paw design is also available, which is a nice alternative if they don't yet have your breed. Passion for Dogs carries earrings, pendants, and brooches and each makes a nice conversation
piece for yourself or a thoughtful gift for a friend.

This is an online and mail-order business that ships worldwide.
Postage is free to the United Kingdom and Europe and is just £1 worldwide, making it quite reasonable to order from anywhere. They are
dedicated to customer satisfaction and they welcome suggestions or

comments. If you're not satisfied with your purchase, you can return it within seven days with the receipt and in its original packaging and condition and they will provide a replacement item or a refund of the cost of the item, whichever you prefer. You are, of course, responsible for the return postage. They do not charge for an item until they are ready to ship.

Allow seven days for processing and delivery in the United Kingdom, ten days in Europe, and fourteen days internationally. If the item you choose isn't in stock, they'll back order it for you. They will e-mail first, to offer you the choice of back ordering or canceling your order if you prefer not to wait.

For information: passionfordogs.co.uk; e-mail: info@passionfordogs .co.uk; Passion for Dogs, Willow Cottage, Cryers Hill Rd., Cryers Hill, Buckinghamshire, HP15 6JS, United Kingdom.

PETLOGIC

With an assortment of wonderful pet products—ranging from foul weather coats to reflective safety vests, a dog collar wallet, crates, backpacks, life jackets, a car booster seat, collapsible bowls, an assortment of fun toys, and more—this online company in New Zealand provides a terrific range of products. They have a 100 percent, satisfaction guaranteed policy. You can return an item within twenty days for a full refund of the purchase price (not the return freight, of course). They will pay the freight on your order when they send it to you.

For information: petlogic.co.nz; e-mail: viv@petlogic.co.nz; telephone: 0800-738-564; fax: (09) 4899-734; Pets by Design, Ltd., P.O. Box 331 259, Takapuna, Auckland, New Zealand.

PETLONDON.COM

This company has some absolutely wonderful items for your dog, including an assortment of whimsical outfits that would be wonderfully amusing for therapy dogs to sport when visiting hospitals or nursing homes. They have a wide range of fashion, accessories, and safety items. You'll find bathrobes for your dog; necklaces; adorable collars and leads; treats; toys; clever dog beds, including one that looks like a car and another that looks like an apple; carriers; and more. They also carry some wonderful items for dog owners, including personalized bags, pins, and fun jewelry.

Their London showroom can be visited by appointment, so call first to make arrangements. They deliver internationally. Items can be exchanged for alternate sizes within seven days of receipt, but they must be in unused condition and in their original packaging. Alternately, PetLondon will issue a credit. Refunds for toys will only be given if the toys are found to be defective. Details of their return policy and how to return packages can be found at their website.

For information: petlondon.com; e-mail: office@petlondon.com; telephone: +44 (0) 800 083 3418; fax: +44 (0) 207 323 2322; PetLondon Ltd., 16 Wigmore St., London W1U 2RF, United Kingdom.

PETPOCKET MEMORIES

This company will take photographs and print them onto a composite card that's not laminated but rather the same size, thickness, and texture as a credit card. They can even print text on the card, so you can add your dog's name, breed, or any information to make it even more meaningful to you. The cards are in full color and will not wear or tear. A large photo can also be converted to create a Petpocket Memory using digital technology and sublimation printers. You can also buy a card holder or minimemory stand. For a small additional charge, the Petpocket Memory can be made into a magnet.

For information: petpocketmemories.com; e-mail: gordon@gpromo .freeserve.co.uk; telephone: 01227-712424 or 07789-401124; Petpocket Memories, 76 Deansway Ave., Sturry, Canterbury, Kent CT2 0NN, United Kingdom.

PETSAFE

Petsafe, a mail-order business, makes made-to-measure, machine-washable, personalized collars and leads. If your dog's tag is lost, he can still have your telephone number embroidered on his collar, which will be clearly visible.

The collars and leashes come in a variety of colors, so you can easily choose one that appeals to you. Petsafe allows you to select both the collar and embroidery colors. Up to twenty characters, including spaces, can be embroidered. Petsafe states that their collars and leashes are strong and durable and are trimmed with brass buckles and clips. The company also carries key fobs and personalized pet beds. You can phone for a free brochure and order by phone, mail, or online. Visit their website to see the products before you order.

For information: petsafe.uk.com; e-mail: sales@petsafe.uk.com; telephone: 01473 738007, or (mobile): 07790 084112; fax: 01473 0738006; Green Farm Trading Petsafe Collars and Leads, The Old Garage, Hall Farm Barns, Hasketon, Woodbridge, Suffolk, 1P13 6JJ, United Kingdom.

TAFF'S PET PLAZA

Taff's Pet Plaza, owned by a master groomer in New Zealand, has a range of supplies for dogs. They have a retail and grooming shop and can also be found at dog shows, which more than makes sense because the owner, Sheila Morris, has been a dog breeder since 1957.

Morris has a mobile shop on the back of a bus that she takes to dog shows; and along with her regular shop, she has a permanent show supply shop at Canterbury Kennel Club's show venue in Christchurch. Morris has been a member of that club for more than forty-six years. She also carries products for cats, birds, and fish. Her company motto is, "If we haven't got it, we will do our best to get it." A visit to the website reveals articles as well as items to buy. You can even find advice on which brushes and combs to buy for which type of coat.

For information: taffspetplaza.co.nz; e-mail: taffs@extra.co.nz; telephone: 03-359 3118; fax: 03-359 5118; Taff's Pet Plaza, 33 Bishopdale Shopping Centre, Christchurch, New Zealand.

2

Health and Grooming

T aking good care of your companion is important because the better you care for him, the longer he'll live and the healthier he'll be. You will both be able to enjoy his quality of life. Two very helpful websites are those of the American Veterinary Medical Association (AVMA) and the American Animal Hospital Association (AAHA). Each has a section especially devoted to pet owners. You can find each respectively at avma.org (click on "Care for Animals") and healthypet .com, which will take you directly to AAHA's pages for pet owners.

HEALTH

Considering health insurance for your dog, physical therapy if it's needed, or sun goggles for those sunny days, dogs have many of the same options today as their owners.

PET HEALTH INSURANCE

Pet health insurance is a fairly new concept that has evolved over the past decade or so. Regular insurance plans or HMOs, like those for people, are available. Obviously, if you opt for the HMO-type plan, use one to which your veterinarian subscribes. Otherwise, you pay your veterinarian and then submit the claim to the insurance company. Usually, these plans cover emergencies. This can save the owner a good deal of money if, for example, the dog got loose and was hit by a car, necessitating hip-replacement surgery. The plans usually cannot be started when the dog is old but must be purchased while your companion is still a puppy or young dog.

If you're a careful saver, the alternative is to open a bank account for your pet and put away money on a regular basis so you will have it available if your dog needs expensive medical care.

Some examples of medical coverage plans available today for pets include the following.

PET ASSURE

This company states that theirs is a comprehensive pet-care program, but it's not insurance. Pet owners receive a 25 percent savings from participating veterinary providers. There are no exclusions for age or preexisting conditions. Food, flea products, routine boarding and grooming, however, are at the veterinarian's discretion. Additional savings from other pet-related merchants and service providers are available.

For information: petassure.com; telephone (toll-free): 888-789-PETS; Pet Assure, 10 South Morris St., Dover, NJ 07801.

PREMIER PET INSURANCE

Premier Pet Insurance has three different plans for your pet, at three different levels of care. Premier Basic covers illness and injury, plus spay/neuter; Premier Value covers most routine care plus spay/neuter, illness, and injury; Premier Choice covers comprehensive care plus spay/neuter, illness, and injury. You choose your own veterinarian with each plan. You pay no enrollment fee. As of this writing, Premier Pet Insurance is not available in Alaska, Arkansas, Hawaii, Idaho, Montana, Nevada, Puerto Rico, South Dakota, or Wyoming. Check with the company periodically to see if any have been added.

For information: ppins.com; telephone (toll-free): 877-774-2273.

VETERINARY PET INSURANCE

Founded in 1990 by veterinarian Jack L. Stephens, Veterinary Pet Insurance boasts of being the number-one pet insurance company in the United States, along with being the nation's oldest. The company was founded to end economic euthanasia and bring affordable pet care to pet owners.

Pet owners can visit any licensed veterinarian in the world, which is a consideration for the individual who travels with his or her pet. Policies cover pets from the age of six weeks and older, with no upper age limit. The policy covers such things as gastric torsion (bloat), diabetes, accidents, heart conditions, kidney problems, and much more. *For information:* petinsurance.com; telephone (toll-free): 800-USA-PETS; Veterinary Pet Insurance, P.O. Box 2344, Brea, CA 92822.

INTERNATIONAL

PET PLAN

Ellenco Enterprises, with insurance underwritten by Lumley General Insurance (New Zealand), offers health insurance plans through New Zealand's largest website that reunites lost pets with their owners (pets onthenet.co.nz). Although you will be billed by the insurance company, when you purchase your pet insurance through the website you will be supporting Pets on the Net's work. The website also helps people find pets available for adoption. The site is free and there is no charge to post a notice about a pet lost anywhere in the world.

The site also contains other interesting features. There are five different pet insurance plans: Classic, Ultra, Premier, Bronze, and Silver. Each offers different levels of coverage. The Bronze and Silver plans cover surgery only, while the others provide both medical and surgical coverage. There's also a design-it-yourself plan. The company offers free coverage for four weeks for puppies ages four to sixteen weeks old.

Order pet tags to help keep the site free. While the insurance is only sold to those who live in New Zealand, they sell tags to anyone, anywhere in the world. The engraved, good-quality metal tags in nice designs are made in New Zealand and cost between $10 and $15 (New

Zealand dollars, which is approximately $5 to $7.50 U.S. dollars). A small extra shipping charge will be added to mail overseas.

For information: petsonthenet.co.nz; e-mail: mail@petsonthenet .co.nz; telephone: (09) 268 6380; fax: (09) 268 6326; Pets on the Net Limited, P.O. Box 16 291, Sandringham, Auckland, New Zealand.

PETCARE PET INSURANCE PROGRAMS

While this company's website clicks through to a company in the United States, it is Canada's number-one provider of pet insurance. Founded in 1998, they are also exclusively endorsed by the Canadian, Ontario, and Quebec Veterinary Medical Associations. They offer several different plans for dogs from the comprehensive to the very basic. Specific details of each plan are available from the company.

For information: petcareinsurance.com; e-mail: info@petcarein surance.com; telephone (toll-free): 866-275-PETS; fax: 866-368-PETS (Phone hours are Monday through Friday, 8 A.M. to midnight, and Saturday, 10 A.M. to 6 P.M., EST.); PetCare Pet Insurance Programs, 710 Dorval Dr., Suite 400, Oakville, ON L6K 3V7, Canada.

PETPLAN

This company won an award from the readers of several magazines as being the best pet insurance plan in the United Kingdom. Dog breeders can arrange for their puppy buyers to get PetPlan's Instant Free Puppy Policies so that new owners will get six weeks of free insurance.

Along with coverage for illness or injury, they also offer third-party liability insurance, if your pet injures someone, and boarding, if you're in the hospital for more than four days; if your pet is lost or stolen, the company will pay for newspaper advertising and a reward. They have other benefits including payment for death from injury or illness or losing a pet as a result of theft or straying if the dog isn't found. And there's a holiday cancellation—visit their website for details. The company also has a charitable trust to provide grants for animal welfare projects.

For information: petplan.co.uk; telephone: 020 8580 8080; fax: 020 8580 8001; PetPlan, Computer House, Great West Rd., Brentford, Middlesex TW8 9DX, United Kingdom.

MEDICATION

Most people buy their pet's flea-control products and prescription medication from their veterinarian. Veterinarians charge less than medical doctors for their services, even though they spend just as many years in college and their education is just as expensive as a medical doctor's. Some of us don't mind the convenience of purchasing medication from our veterinarian whose expenses are higher because he or she must maintain his or her own hospital as well, which includes staffing and medical equipment.

Other people prefer to order via mail order to save money. You will need a written prescription from your veterinarian to do this. Keep in mind that for the average layperson, giving vaccinations at home to save money is a classic case of penny-wise and pound foolish. If your dog has a reaction, you will in no way be prepared to handle it and you will need to make an emergency trip to the veterinarian for assistance, hoping you can get there in time.

Dogs, like their owners, might require physical therapy from time to time. A variety of services and treatments are available for our canine companions.

CANINE HYDROTHERAPY AND ALTERNATIVE TREATMENTS

Canine hydrotherapy allows dogs to get the exercise they need to recover from injuries, with as little stress as possible, using water exercises much as people would. It can help with flexibility and range of motion. Many dogs are physically active and can have sports injuries as well as other physical problems, such as arthritis or orthopedic conditions; alternative treatments that might include hydrotherapy can be beneficial to your dog.

LA PAW SPA

Redmond, Washington, is home to La Paw Spa, which is surrounded by organic gardens and picnic areas, adding to the therapeutic atmosphere of a gently healthy mind and body. La Paw Spa, established in 1996, was the first warm-water spa of its kind in the Northwest.

La Paw Spa features a holistically maintained warm-water therapy pool. Range of motion work and other non-weight-bearing exercise, swimming, and warm-water massage can be beneficial to a dog who has an injury or chronic condition such as dysplasia. The powerful swim jets can help build and maintain muscle for a dog who has been paralyzed. La Paw Spa's mission statement is, "To assist canine and human companion alike in physical, emotional, and spiritual healing. To help unfold the blessings and gifts hidden in hardship, disabilities, and the aging process. To be present and lovingly available to both during these times."

They will customize a program for your dog in collaboration with your veterinarian. The therapists at La Paw Spa are fully licensed and trained in physical healing and fitness.

For information: lapawspa.com; e-mail: cindy@lapawspa.com; telephone: 425-222-WOOF.

TOPS VETERINARY REHAB

TOPS considers itself to be the most advanced veterinary rehabilitation center in the United States. The facility was opened in 1998 by Dr. Laurie McCauley, who lectures both nationally and internationally on veterinary rehabilitation. They have clients who fly in from around the United States and from other countries as well. Their goal is to speed healing while minimizing pain. Their mission statement is, "At TOPS Veterinary Rehab, our mission is to improve the quality of life for our patients by providing the best available rehabilitation and pain management services in a warm, comfortable, caring atmosphere. Our goal is not only to improve the physical condition of the patient, but to strengthen the pet-owner bond as well."

TOPS offers hydro-treadmill therapy, the world's first one for dogs; therapeutic ultrasound; cryotherapy; neuromuscular stimulation; acupuncture; aquatic bioelectric therapy; animal chiropractic; and more. Your dog is evaluated by a licensed veterinarian, certified in both veterinary acupuncture and animal chiropractic. TOPS also employs a licensed physical therapist to provide a comprehensive treatment plan.

The facility has been expanded to include two underwater treadmills. They have two state-of-the-art therapy pools; each includes an automatic sanitizer, an ozonator, a mineral purifier, and a filtration system for a 40' by 30' swimming pool. The 5' by 7' pools are complete with everything to ensure they remain as safe and sanitary as possible. They also offer sports medicine to help prevent injuries before they can happen. TOPS Veterinary Rehabilitation is located in the north suburbs of Chicago, approximately thirty-five miles north of O'Hare International Airport.

For information: tops-vet-rehab.com; e-mail: drmc@tops-vet-rehab .com; telephone: 847-548-9470; fax: 847-548-9472; TOPS Veterinary Rehab, 1440 E. Belvidere Rd., Grayslake, IL 60030.

INTERNATIONAL

AMBERCO CANINE HYDROTHERAPY

Amberco Canine Hydrotherapy in England believes that their treatments can not only be beneficial for injuries, arthritis, or orthopedic conditions but for obesity, fitness training, and general convalescence as well. It is the warmth as well as the pressure and buoyancy of the water that have a positive effect. Some of the benefits are relief of pain, swelling, and stiffness, as well as promoting relaxation, joint mobilization, muscle strengthening and restoration, increased range of motion of affected joints, improved circulation, and cardiovascular fitness.

All dogs are swum by appointment and by veterinary referral only. Their hydrotherapy pool was custom designed and built and has two antiswim jets, which are adjustable for both flow rate and direction. Underwater lighting assists in the observation of limb movement. To prevent bacteria, they use an ozonator and a saltwater chlorinator. Tests are conducted several times a day to ensure the chemical and pH balance of the pool are maintained at proper levels. Dogs enter and exit the pool by use of ramps and an electrically powered hoist.

They also have the first canine water walker in England. This is an underwater treadmill with variable speed control, and the depth of the water, which is heated, can be quickly and accurately adjusted, which allows it to be used by different size dogs. It also helps increase or decrease the water resistance.

Their hydro spa was designed and built with multiple compart-ments to accommodate dogs of various sizes and shapes. The hydro spa has a massaging effect. If your dog is dirty when he arrives or you want to shower him off after his session, a warm-water shower is available. Whether or not you use the shower, you can use the drying room, which has towels and a handheld electric dryer. Dog coats are avail-able for old, frail dogs or for those who need pampering. The coats can be rented for the duration of the course of treatment or made to measure for purchase. They're reversible and are made to help dry the dog as well as keep him warm.

They have several treatment programs available. More detailed information can be found at their website. Canine Hydrotherapy has a working relationship with a remedial and manipulative therapist who works with humans as well as animals and is a member of the Canine Hydrotherapy Association.

For information: amberco-canine-centres.co.uk; e-mail: swimdogs@amberco-canine-centres.co.uk; telephone: 01761 451580; fax: 01761 453599; Canine Hydrotherapy, Paulwood Barn, Temple Cloud, Som-erset BS39 5DQ, U.K. (Center hours are Monday through Friday, 9 A.M. to 6 P.M., and Saturdays, 10 A.M. to 4 P.M. They are closed on Sundays and bank holidays.)

PET RAMPS AND STAIRS AND OTHER HELPFUL AIDS

When they get older, some dogs need a little extra help getting in and out of the car or up on their favorite chairs and beds. Sometimes it's arthritis, for other dogs (younger ones, as well), hip dysplasia or a severely luxating patellar (kneecap) can cause some mobility issues. And some owners are concerned about a very small dog being acciden-tally injured in a fall from the car, SUV, truck, or furniture. Addition-ally, you might want to provide added protection to your dog's sensitive eyes. Many options are available to assist these dogs and their owners. While you might find some of these products at various retailers, you're better off dealing directly with the company for the latest information on the product.

DOGGLES

Doggles is protective eyewear for your dog. No joke. Doggles' shatter-proof and antifog lenses will help protect your dog's eyes by blocking 100 percent of UV rays, as well as prevent wind and dirt from getting into the dog's eyes. Doggles wrap around and are secured with elastic, providing your dog with eye protection from any sort of damage from stray light or foreign objects. They completely enclose the eyes for protection. Along with the original Doggles, they now have ILS—Interchange Lens System. You can choose different lenses in different colors for your dog's Doggles. Two adjustable elastic straps keep Doggles on securely during any activity. They come in sizes from XS through XL. Doggles also has other products including a pet sunscreen, car window shades, and an annual Doggles calendar. And you can buy lens cleaner and a replacement carrying pouch. Their website has a listing of stores that carry Doggles internationally, along with tips and tricks.

For information: doggles.com; e-mail: info@doggles.com; telephone (toll-free): 866-DOGGLES or (local): 209-295-2933; fax: 209-295-2934; Midnight Creations, LLC/Doggles, 505-1 S. State Hwy. 49 #284, Jackson, CA 95642-2552.

PAW STEPS™

This ramp is lightweight (less than seven pounds) and comes in various sizes. It is meant for use in the home to help your dog gain access to chairs, beds, sofas, as well as cars. While it's meant mainly for smaller dogs, Paw Steps supports more than 120 pounds. The ramp also makes it convenient for older people; rather than having to lift their dog onto furniture or into the car, they can use the ramp. It requires no assembly and comes with a lifetime warranty. The ramp is available in two sizes: small and large. You can purchase a separate extension for the large one.

For information: pawsteps.com; e-mail: pawsteps@aol.com; telephone (toll-free): 877-4-PAWSTEP; Paw Steps, P.O. Box 3655, Laguna Beach, CA 91701.

PETSTEP

If you prefer a lightweight, portable ramp to help your dog get in and out of your car, van, truck, or SUV, PetSTEP has a ribbed, nonslip surface with a rubberized coating. It swings open or closed, requires no special setup or hardware, and it holds any weight dog. It also floats in water, so it could be used in swimming pools and boats. It won't rust or corrode and can be washed with soap and water. Optional aluminum legs will allow you to turn it into a table. This ramp has the ASPCA's approval. *For information:* petstep.com; e-mail: info@petstep.com; telephone (toll-free): 877-PetSTEP or (local): 650-960-1297; fax: 650-960-8296; PetSTEP, Inc., warehouse: 790 Dubuque Ave., South San Francisco, CA 94080; mailing address: P.O. Box 2784, South San Francisco, CA 94080.

TWISTEP®

Twistep is, literally, a step that attaches to the hitch receiver on your SUV or truck and stows away under the bumper. It holds up to five hundred pounds, so even the giant breeds can safely use it. It has a nonslip surface and a corrosion-resistant coating.
For information: twistep.com; e-mail: info@otllc.com; telephone (toll-free): 888-284-7742 or (local): 208-284-6830; fax: 206-284-8739; Twistep, OT LLC, 2212 Queen Anne Ave. N. PMB 712, Seattle, WA 98109.

INTERNATIONAL

DOG RAMPS™

These ramps are nonslip, handcrafted, and the manufacturer claims they won't scratch your vehicle. The ramps are carpeted and sturdy and will help any elderly dog or ailing dog of any size who needs some assistance getting in and out of the car, van, or truck. They can also be used near furniture without causing harm because no nails or staples are used in the construction of the ramps.
For information: dogramps.on.ca; telephone (toll-free): 877-206-6636; Dog Ramps, 2885 Altona Rd., Locust Hill, ON L0H 1J0 Canada.

DOGGIE WHEELCHAIRS

Some dogs can become paralyzed for a variety of reasons and might be unable to use their back legs and must drag them when they walk.

Some companies make doggie wheelchairs to aid these dogs and allow them more mobility. The hind legs go into the cart, and the dog uses her front legs while the back legs are brought along with the wheels. Some dogs do quite well with these. The dog will need to have strong front legs and body to support this and the dog will need a place to lie down and rest if she's in the cart for a long period of time. You will also want to monitor your dog to ensure that she isn't running so fast that the cart falls over. Never leave your pet unsupervised while in the cart.

DOGGON' WHEELS

This company sells wheelchairs, quad chairs, front extensions, support slings, and other products such as paw protectors and doggie diapers. Their saddle support system is designed to allow the dog to urinate and defecate while in the wheelchair or when used separately. The wheelchair will be built for a custom fit. Some smaller dogs can lie down while in their wheelchair but all dogs must be taken out of the wheelchair to rest.

For information: doggon.com; e-mail: doggon@doggon.com (Qualified staff is available to answer questions Monday through Friday, 8 A.M. to 4 P.M., MST.); telephone (toll-free): 800-736-4466 or (local): 406-222-5574; fax (toll-free): 888-0236-4239 or (local): 406-222-5790; Doggon' Wheels, P.O. Box 1503, Livingston, MT 59047.

EDDIE'S WHEELS FOR PETS

These wheelchairs for disabled dogs are custom made to each dog's measurements. The company founders' dog was disabled by disc disease, so they built her a cart. She was ultimately rehabilitated. Since that time, the cart has evolved into a lightweight aluminum cart with a welded frame, machined fittings, stainless-steel hardware, and molded closed-cell foam padding. The company also builds front wheel carts for dogs that have lost one or both front limbs or have front limb mobility problems. The company states candidly that the front wheel carts are more difficult to use and require a serious time commitment from the owner because both must train for its use, which requires both motivation and patience.

For information: eddieswheels.com; e-mail: ed@eddieswheels.com; telephone (toll-free): 888-211-2700 or (local): 413-625-0033; fax: 413-625-8428; Eddie's Wheels for Pets, 347 Little Mohawk Rd., Shelburne Falls, MA 01370.

K-9 CARTS

The original K-9 Carts, which are described as wheelchairs for mobility-impaired pets, were designed by veterinary orthopedic specialist Dr. Lincoln Parkes more than thirty-six years ago. Their slogan is "Improving the quality of life—because disability shouldn't deny choices." The company's website can be accessed in English, Spanish, German, and French and provides a lot of information, including nursing care and tips. Their products section also contains nursing-care products for your dog, as well as the K-9 Carts, and WalkAbout Harnesses to help you help your dog walk. You can also find information on the K-9 E-Z Lift to help you assist your large dog who might need temporary, handheld support.

For information: k9carts.com; e-mail: wheels@k9carts.com; telephone (toll-free): 800-578-6960 or (local): 360-675-1808; fax: 360-675-1809; K-9 Cart Company, 656 S.E. Bayshore Dr., Suite #2, Oak Harbor, WA 98277. (Office hours are Monday through Friday, 9 A.M. to 5 P.M., PST.)

TTOUCH

TTouch is a method of massage begun by Linda Tellington-Jones, a horse person who has carried this method to virtually every species. It uses circular motions and is like massage. It is meant to activate cell function and the TTouch technique is used in healing injuries and with behavior problems. Practitioners are around the world.

CRICKET MARA

Cricket Mara of The Pawsitive Dog, Inc., is as passionate about dogs as her partner, Karla McCoy. She is a certified Tellington TTouch Practitioner for companion animals. She works with private clients and is also available to give workshops and demonstrations for interested groups.

For information: pawsitivedog.com; e-mail: info@pawsitivedog.com; telephone: 309-699-6935. The Pawsitive Dog, P.O. Box 185, Groveland, IL 61535.

DEBBY POTTS

TTouch is available at the Integrated Animal in Portland, Oregon. Debby Potts not only practices TTouch, but the Integrated Animal hosts workshops for those interested in learning to do it themselves. She and her partner, animal communicator Lauren McCall, have held more than fifty-four workshops, attended by more than seven hundred people in the United States and Japan. McCall is also a TTouch practitioner and former executive director of the TTEAM and Tellington TTouch organization. (You can find more about McCall in Chapter 8 under "Animal Communicators.") Potts and McCall point out that people often turn to TTouch when they want to improve an animal's health or change a behavior pattern. Potts is a recognized TTEAM and TTouch instructor with more than fourteen years' experience. She is a licensed veterinary technician and speaks at international conferences and workshops and works privately with people in the United States, Europe, Japan, and South Africa. She also holds second and fourth degree Reiki and has had craniosacral therapy training. She is a member of the Association of Pet Dog Trainers (APDT). Private consultations and workshops are available.

For information: http://integratedanimal.com; e-mail: info@integrated animal.com; telephone: 503-704-7499; fax: 503-293-7298; the Integrated Animal, 8435 S.W. Carmel Ct., Portland, OR 97223.

LINDA TELLINGTON-JONES

Tellington Touch, better known as TTouch, began in the 1960s with horses when Linda Tellington-Jones developed her Equine Awareness method. She has since brought it to virtually every other species. TTouch is very commonly used on dogs and cats and some use it for wildlife. The formal TTeam approach began in the 1970s. It is well worth reading Linda Tellington-Jones's background on her website. The philosophy of TTouch and TTeam is, "to honor the role of animals as our teachers; to bring awareness to the importance of animals in our lives; to encourage harmony, cooperation, and trust between humans and animals and amongst humans; to recognize the individual learning process of every human and animal; to respect each animal as an individual; to teach interspecies communication through the TTouch; and to work with animals using understanding rather than dominance." You can find a practitioner directory on the website to find one near you. And for those who would like to become a TTouch practitioner, a certification program is available. The website lists centers in other countries as well as a newsletter and an Internet discussion group.

For information: http://tteam-ttouch.com; e-mail: info@ttouch.com; telephone (toll-free in the United States): 800-854-8326 or (in Canada): 250-545-2336; fax (in the United States): 505-455-7233 or (in Canada): 250-545-9116; TTeam and TTouch International, P.O. Box 3793, Santa Fe, NM 87506. In Canada, 5435 Rochdell Rd., Vernon, BC V1B 3E8, Canada.

DOG SPAS

Owners treat their pets as beloved family members, so why shouldn't the canine member of the family go to a spa, get massages, and enjoy special treatment!

DOG DAY CAFÉ & SPA

Hermitage, Tennessee, is home to the Dog Day Café & Spa. This is not just a doggie bakery or a place to shop, although it does include both. This is an all-encompassing experience. Clicker training is offered here as are canine aromatherapy, Bach Flower remedies, and massage. They have an agility area and all sorts of things to buy for your canine friend and yourself. (Fat-free, flavored coffee is also available to purchase and brew at home.) You and your dog can have a treat together in the café. They also have day care for owners who don't want to leave their dog home alone or crated all day but would prefer to have her supervised by someone while she plays with other dogs. You can also arrange for spa treatments while your dog is at day care. They also offer a Friday night social club for a small fee (and advance reservations). The social club is set up for dogs and owners to get together, which can be very nice for dogs who don't have canine playmates at home.

At the Dog Day Café & Spa, you'll find all things for all doggies and their people, including garden sculptures of dogs and cats, fancy collars for your dog, collar charms, treats, interactive toys to stimulate your dog's mind and keep him too busy to get into mischief, and much, much more with a fair guarantee and return policy. In keeping with their positive attitude, they also support their local animal shelters, the Nashville Humane Association and the Wilson County Humane Society. They are also at Dog Days in the Park at Central Park in Nashville, as well as at the Bark in the Park in Lebanon, which benefits Wilson County Humane Society.

For information: dogdaycafe.com; e-mail: info@dogdaycafe.com; telephone: 615-874-8527; fax: 615-874-2434; Dog Day Café & Spa, 3646 Central Pike, Hermitage, TN 37076. (Hours are Monday through Friday, 7 A.M. to 6 P.M., CST.)

GROOMING

Grooming your dog is an essential component in her health care. Not only will it help to keep her skin and hair or fur healthier but it will provide time for you two to be together to bond even more closely. Plus, of course, it will give you an opportunity to go over your dog regularly to see if there are any lumps or bumps on the skin, or any fleas, flea dirt, ticks, and so forth. If your dog's coat is too much for you to manage at home beyond brushing and combing, you can take your dog to a professional pet groomer.

Grooming equipment can be found at virtually any pet supply store. One item you might not have considered, however, is an elevated dog bath:

BOOSTER BATH®

The Booster Bath puts your dog at a level that will allow you to protect your back while you wash your dog. It is a portable washing tub although it does weigh about twenty-three pounds, but it can support several hundred pounds. The tub and its pedestal are made of quarter-inch-thick, ultraviolet stabilized, high-density polyethylene. This should mean that it will be durable and last a long time. The bottom of the pedestal has rubber on it to keep it from sliding. The tub and pedestal are held together with noncorroding, stainless steel screws. A rubberized mat at the bottom of the tub prevents your dog from slipping or sliding. It also has a caddy that holds shampoo, conditioner, and brush, keeping them handy during the bath. It has a leash restraint for your dog, and the exit hose is six feet long, so you can wash the dog in one area and dispose of the water in another.

If you have more than one dog, or just want to save yourself the strain of leaning over the bathtub or want something more than hosing down the dog in the backyard, you might want to check out the Booster Bath.

For information: pawsforthought.com; e-mail: sales@dogbath.com; telephone (toll-free): 888-494-4004; fax: 619-596-8137; Paws for Thought, 2163 Cumbre Pl., San Diego, CA 92020.

INTERNATIONAL

DOGS IN THE CITY

This is a full-service pet grooming salon in the Vancouver area of British Columbia. They will do everything from a basic bath and brushing to hand-stripping of Terriers. Dogs in the City uses the finest quality shampoos for your companion, and they strive to make it a comfortable experience for your dog in a safe environment. Their goal is to make the experience a positive one so your dog will want to return.

For information: dogsinthecity.ca; telephone: 604-299-0580; Dogs in the City, 4609 Hastings St., Unit 1, Burnaby, BC V5C 2K6, Canada. (Hours are Tuesday through Saturday, 8:30 A.M. to 4:30 P.M. Like most salons for humans, they're closed on Sunday and Monday.)

3

Feed Me!

F ood. It's one of the highlights of your dog's day, whether we're talking about a meal or discussing special treats. Your dog depends on you for a complete and balanced diet that will keep him healthy for his entire lifetime. If you travel with your companion, he's going to need a diet—along with lots of fresh water—that will keep him healthy on the road. If you're heading out on a day trip, you can bring along a bottle of your own tap water, if that's what he drinks at home.

But for longer trips, it will be safer to carry bottled water. The bacteria in water will change from place to place, which might very well upset your dog's digestive tract. Why take a chance? He'll be very happy with bottled water, and you can find folding water dishes available for travel.

And don't forget to adjust your dog's diet to his activity level. Petdiets.com is a great place to get really good information about pet nutrition. Treats should be just that: treats. They should be made from quality ingredients and not fed in large quantities.

While some specialty bakeries have brick and mortar stores that you can visit, if you surf the Internet, you can find some interesting food-related sites. Many of the pet food companies offer free samples. Because it would be impossible to know which samples would be available at any given time, these are best accessed by visiting the individual pet food company's website. You can find them quite easily by either using the company name or by going to a search engine and entering the words *pet food*.

Here are some lesser known places where you can find treats for your companion:

AUNT V'S™

Aunt V's has handy items—such as cooling neck wraps—along with cookies for your dog or cat. Fresh-baked dog treats made with wholesome ingredients, such as carrots and oats, include K-9 Crunch, which comes packaged in "Tin Tie-Lined Bakery Bags" to keep them as fresh as possible. Aunt V's Nutritious Training Treats for Dogs and Cats are made with pure dehydrated turkey liver. They're all natural with no preservatives or additives and come in a resealable pouch. They will ship outside the United States.

For information: auntv.com; e-mail (orders): vanessa@auntv.com or auntv@mindspring.com; telephone: 615-969-4241; Aunt V's, P.O. Box 235, Arrington, TN 37014.

BARBARA'S CANINE CAFÉ

All-natural dog treats are featured at Barbara's Canine Café. They have no preservatives, fillers, artificial coloring, sodium, sugars, or added fat. The café states that they have arrived at their selection of treats with their own trial and error and taste tests done by the North Carolina State University food science department and private laboratories and through consultation with veterinarians. Along with the biscuits, they have treat trays to use as a "pawty" favor, dog celebration "pawty" cakes that are personalized and come in various shapes and sizes, and celebration gift baskets for those special doggie occasions. They also have a biscuit-of-the-month club. Online, you'll find a message board, news and events, and a picture gallery among other things.

For information: k9treat.com; telephone (toll-free): 888-K-TREAT or (local): 704-LUV-DOGS; fax: 704-889-4931; Barbara's Canine Café,

315 Main St., P.O. Box 718, Pineville, NC 28134. (Café hours are Monday through Friday, 11 A.M. to 6 P.M.; Saturday, 10 A.M. to 5 P.M.; and Sunday by appointment only ["for socially challenged canines"].)

BARKERS' BAKERY

Barkers' Bakery has created a nutritious dog treat that will appeal to humans, so watch where you put these or some of your two-legged family members might mistakenly consume them, leaving nothing for your dog! Believe it or not, they make Barkers' Biscotti. They have no artificial flavorings or preservatives, sugar, salt, or pesticides. The flavors are chicken pot pie, hearty beef stew, zesty cheese and garlic, Chicago deep-dish pizza, and peanut butter.

For information: dogtreat.com; e-mail: info@dogtreat.com; telephone: 847-356-6750; fax: 847-356-6750; Barkers' International Gourmet Bakery, Ltd., 736 N. Western Ave., Suite 209, Lake Forest, IL 60045.

THE BONE APPETIT TREAT SHOP™

Located in Syosset, New York, Bone Appetit Treat Shop caters to pets, but the owners claim that you could eat the treats too because the ingredients are healthy. They have an assortment of goodies, some of them arranged in variety packs. One such offering is packed on a Frisbee. Their tasty trays include one consisting of doggie cannoli and another with cinnamon Roll-Me-Overs. Pup Cigars, Howling Bagels, and Bark-B-Que Ribs are among the clever names of treats available here. They also sell collectibles, eyeglass holders, a board game, and a number of other items.

For information: tastypettreats.com; telephone: 516-921-6694; The Bone Appetit Treat Shop, 340 Jericho Turnpike, Syosset, NY 11791.

CANINE COOKIE COMPANY™

The treats at Canine Cookie Company are baked-in-the-oven goodies that are made from all-natural premium ingredients. The treats are sweetened with honey and molasses; they do not use salt, nor do they add processed sugar. Bagged treats include Bon Bons™, Cinnamon Dunkers™, P'nut Puppies™, Canine Ahoys™, Love Bites™, Snicker Pooches™, and more. Lite treats include Veggie Bone™ and

Liva Bone™. They also offer training treats: Cheeze Bits and Liver Slivers.

You can purchase gift baskets, some in a bone-shaped tin; others are in a canister, fireplug, or doghouse, making for an attractive presentation. You can also find Christmas tins and Christmas baskets. Personalized gift cards are available for the baskets at an additional charge. They also have a dog-treat-of-the-month club. They sell their own cookbook, which comes with a stainless steel cookie cutter in the shape of a dog bone. And they welcome wholesale accounts.

For information: canine-cookie.com; e-mail: treat@dbcity.net; telephone (toll-free): 888-572-5572 (Phone orders are taken Monday through Friday, 7 A.M. to 6 P.M., CST.) or (local): 512-267-9729; Canine Cookie Company, 21527 Paine Ave., Lago Vista, TX 78645.

CANINE CRAVINGS™ BAKERY FOR DOGS

Canine Cravings Bakery for Dogs makes healthy treats for dogs that are not only tested by the company dog but by the owner as well. The biscuits come in four sizes, from training treats to large cookies. They also come in a variety of shapes—stars, bones, and hearts and special shapes—as well as Carob Chip Woofies, Pea-Mutt Butter Nutters, and Bow Wow Beef and Bow Wow Chicken flavors.

For information: caninecravings.com; e-mail: feedback@caninecravings.com; telephone: 919-841-1401 (Phone orders are taken Monday through Friday, 10 A.M. to 5 P.M., EST.); Canine Cravings, 9650 Strickland Rd., Suite 103-173, Raleigh, NC 27615.

CHIEN LUNATIQUE

A French bakery for dogs? Why not? Chien Lunatique calls itself a canine *boulangerie* and boutique. With the idea of creating an online bakery for dogs but not knowing what shape it would take, the owners of Chien Lunatique were inspired during a walk through Boston, when they spotted a French novelty plaque near the doorbell of an elegant townhouse.

They refer to themselves as a "virtual bakery for the canine gourmand." All of their baked goods are made without sugar, preservatives, or artificial flavors or coloring. They use the finest ingredients and state that their biscuits are best if used within thirty days of receiving them. Among their biscuits are Chicken Pâté, Foie Gras, Mimolette Herb, and Signature Grand. In their patisserie section, you'll find Canine Madeleines (dusted with trace amounts of confectioners' sugar) and Caniche Petit Fours, both of which should be used within seven days of receiving them. The Caniche Petit Fours should be kept frozen or refrigerated. Specific instructions are at the website, along with ingredients for all baked goods.

They can accommodate premium gift and party orders if you and your dog are celebrating a special occasion. Samplers and e-gifts are also available. They have a boutique for special items for you and your dog, which is also available online, canine featherbeds included. Requested items are shipped within one day of receiving the order. Returns are accepted if they are notified within a week of receiving the items. Club Boulangerie is able to ship internationally as well as within the United States.

Club Boulangerie is for regular customers who want baked goods delivered on a regular basis as well as special birthday offers and special promotions as well as invitations to special tastings and trunk shows.

For information: chienlunatique.com; e-mail (general assistance): customerservice@chienlunatique.com, (feedback): feedback@chien lunatique.com, or (orders): domesticorders@chienlunatique.com, internationalorders@chienlunatique.com, wholesaleenquiries@chien lunatique.com; telephone and fax (toll-free): 877-270-2409; Chien Lunatique, 167 Milk St., Number 248, Boston, MA 02109.

CIAO! BOW WOW

Ciao! Bow Wow's spokesmodel and taste tester is a Cardigan Welsh Corgi named Mame. They feature handmade and hand-cut treats made in small batches using natural, healthy, and human-grade ingredients. Nothing artificial is added, nor is salt or sugar used. They will custom make treats for clients with special needs like allergies. They have a variety of treats available—for cats and horses as well as for dogs. And you can purchase custom packages for holidays, birthdays, and other events.

If you're not happy with the products, you can e-mail Mame, who will have her owner and chef refund your money. Among the treats available are Peanut Butter–Oatmeal dog-shaped cookies or "pup-cakes," Holy Mackerels for dogs or kitties, beef bone–shaped biscuits, and training treats. A gift assortment is also available. Ingredients for each treat are listed on the website.

For information: ciaobowwow.com; e-mail: mel@ciaobowwow.com or mame@ciaobowwow.com; telephone: 978-499-9417; Ciao! Bow Wow, 45 Forrester St., Newburyport, MA 01950.

CULINARY TAILS

If you want to make something for your dog and help a good cause while you're at it, here's an opportunity. *Culinary Tails* is the project of both Whidbey Animals Improvement Foundation (WAIF) (who run the local shelter) and Free Exercise Time for Canines & Their Humans (FETCH) (who established and maintain Whidbey Island's five off-leash parks). The book contains both recipes and whimsy from Whidbey Island.

The cookbook retails for $19.95 per copy, and all proceeds go towards furthering the missions of Whidbey's animal welfare organizations. *Culinary Tails* can be purchased from local retailers if you're in that area of Washington State, or you can order it online from either organization's website.

For information: waif.org or whidbey.com/fetch.

DOGGIE DE LITES®, INC.

If you're thinking that a doggie baking business can turn into a whole-sale company, you're right on target. Doggie de Lites's, natural gourmet dog treats is a case in point. Their biscuits come in twenty-one pack-ages (including one packed with a Frisbee to work off those treats) and six flavors: peanut butter and wheat germ, parmesan cheese, honey and oats, carob, liver, and mint. The liver treats are square while all others come in a bone shape. They have no added preservatives or artificial flavors, yet they are reported to have a shelf life of at least a year.

This family business was started to find treats for the family's two miniature long-haired Dachshunds. You can now find Doggie de Lites at pet shops, gift shops, websites, some department stores, natural food stores, regular grocery chains, and warehouse clubs. Theirs is a wholesale business and they're now exporting to Japan with Japanese stickers on the packages. They do make exceptions to their wholesale-only policy and will ship a case of twelve packages to a consumer if no retailer in his or her area carries the product. They can bake ten thousand pounds a day with one shift and twice that with their second shift. Some of their packaging and all of the labeling, packing, and shipping are handled by handicapped adults in a supervised facility. *For information:* doggiedelites.com; e-mail: doggiedelites@aol.com; telephone (toll-free): 800-988-3596 or (local): 770-888-8226; fax: 770-888-8227; Doggie de Lites, Inc., 4555 Mansell Rd., Suite 300, Alpharetta, GA 30022.

DOGMA GOURMET DOG BAKERY & BOUTIQUE

Arlington, Virginia, in the Washington, D.C., area is home to Dogma Gourmet Dog Bakery & Boutique where they make fresh-baked dog treats daily. Gift items and other dog products are also available and, of course, dogs are welcome. The store has bulletin boards for services, lost pets, adoptions, dog training, dog walkers, and more. Dog owners are invited to come with their dogs and talk about—dogs! The owners are happy to make the store a focal point of the pet community in the D.C. area. Customers can proudly hang photos of their pets on another board in the store or on their website, where you can also find discussion boards. Dogma also carries products for cats and their owners.

The doggie treats have delightful names such as Banana Bis-Scottie, Bubba Bites, Carob Dough Mutts, Gar-Lick Cheese Bites, Happy Hydrant, Pupkin Cookies, Snicker Poodles, and more. Ingredients of each type of treat are listed at the website. It's recommended that the treats be kept in the refrigerator to keep them fresher longer. *For information:* dogmabakery.com; e-mail (owner Mary Hogan): mary@dogmabakery.com; telephone: 703-237-5070; fax: 703-237-

5089; Dogma Dog Bakery & Boutique, 2445 North Harrison St., North Arlington, VA 22207. (Store hours are Sunday, 11 A.M. to 4 P.M.; Tuesday through Friday, 10 A.M. to 7 P.M.; and Saturday, 9 A.M. to 6 P.M., EST. They are closed on Monday.)

FIDO FOOD FAIR

The first of the doggie delis, Chicago's Fido Food Fair has been making gourmet dog treats, cookies, and bakery and deli goods since 1979. They also do canine birthday parties and other dog parties.

It all began when Gloria Lissner—inventor and founder of the first doggie deli, called Famous Fido's Doggie Deli—began to bake and sell the world's first gourmet canine treats in a small grooming shop on Chicago's north side.

Human-quality ingredients are used and no animal products. While it's fun to visit Fido Food Fair in Chicago, you can order the treats online if you live too far from the deli. The choices include doggie sampler, party platter, Fido treat jar, Tub-o-Bones, and more.

A two-week advance notice is required for parties at the store, which are held on Saturdays between 11 A.M. and 5 P.M. and last approximately one hour. Party prices are per dog and the doggie birthday party includes party favors, appetizers, entrée, dessert, and after dinner mints. You may bring food for your dog. Telephone to book your party.

Birthday cakes are baked from cornbread, garlic, and cream cheese with lots of cookies on top as well as your dog's name. The cakes come in two sizes and require a one-day advance notice. Cakes are too fragile to be shipped and must be picked up for parties at home. Cheesecakes are available in one size but two flavors. You can choose from cheddar cheese or peanut butter.

For information: fidofoodfair.com; e-mail: fido@jaske.net; telephone: 773-506-9063; Fido Food Fair, 5418 N. Clark St., Chicago, IL 60640.

FI-DOUGH

This doggie bakery in Boston is also a grooming shop, a place to relax and talk about dogs, and a place to shop for assorted items for your canine companion. Assorted biscuit treats include Canadian Unbacon, Corn Bones, french fries, Snowballs, pretzel sticks, and Royal Snaps. You can also get a mixed sampler pack. They offer truffles, peanut butter and carob hearts, and more. There are also gift baskets for new puppies and assorted gift packages that include treats and doggie items. They also sell bedding; boutique items like clocks, toys, canine apparel; and more.

You can sign up for their free newsletter (past issues are archived at their website). They often advertise a contest in the newsletter, and you might win a Fi-Dough gift certificate.

Fi-Dough strives to ship all orders within twenty-four hours. All products are guaranteed against all manufacturer defects. The exception is plush toys because, obviously, that's an item that can always be destroyed by a dog. You must, of course, assume the cost of return postage for any item you're sending back. There is limited grooming shuttle to Somerville.

For information: fidough.com; e-mail: fidoughpet@aol.com; telephone: 617-661-FIDO or 617-661-PAWS. *Store locations:* Fi-Dough Boston, 103 Charles St., Boston, MA; telephone: 617-723-3266. (Store hours are Sunday, noon to 5 P.M.; Monday through Friday, 11 A.M. to 7 P.M.; and Saturday, 9 A.M. to 6 P.M., EST.) Grooming is by appointment. Fi-Dough Somerville, 70E Beacon St., Somerville, MA; telephone: 617-661-3436 or 617-661-7297. (Store hours are Monday, noon to 6 P.M.; Tuesday and Thursday, 9 A.M. to 6 P.M.; Wednesday, Friday, and Saturday, 9 A.M. to 6 P.M.)

THE GOURMET DOG

This doggie bakery is located in charming Newport, Rhode Island. They specialize in dog biscuits and cakes but also carry other items for your canine companion, such as collars, leashes, water bowls, toys, and items for the proud owner like specialty sweaters and breed-specific merchandise. They even have items for your feline friends.

Treats are baked fresh daily and include such cookies as Cross Ants, Pinwheels, Bagels, and Carrots. Fancy pastries include Peanut Butter Turnover and Slice of Heaven. They cater pet parties and also make special occasion cakes, each one made to order, for events such as birthdays, "barkmitzhfahs," and weddings.

For information: thegourmetdog.com; e-mail: thegourmetdog@the gourmetdog.com; telephone: 401-841-9301; fax: 401-841-5606; The Gourmet Dog, 476B Thames St., Newport, RI.

GREAT DOG BAKERY™

Chef Daryl, the owner of Great Dog Bakery, got the idea for his shop while attending the School of Culinary Arts in Atlanta. His first treats were named after his Jack Russell Terrier, Cosmo. Along with a shop in Portland, Oregon, there's also a website for online orders.

An interesting array of treats is available, from those for breakfast time like Barkin' Bagels and Canine Carob Muffins, to Super Treats like Chicken Pup Pie and Turkey Meatballs. They offer biscuits (including Lolli-Pups), of course, and canine cakes including those for special occasions, and "New Yorkie" cheesecakes. The Great Dog Bakery offers a treat-of-the month club. You can also find recipes online from the *Great Dog Bakery Recipe Book*.

Stating that only the finest and freshest quality ingredients are used, and having Cosmo as the official taste tester, Great Dog Bakery stands behind their products with a personal guarantee. And you can join Cosmo's Corner online to receive special offers, recipes you can make at home, and if you add your pet's name and birthday, she or he will receive a birthday greeting.

For information: greatdogbakery.com; e-mail: info@greatdogbakery .com; telephone (toll-free): 877-292-1113 or (local): 503-292-1111; fax: 503-292-7677; Great Dog headquarters and store, 7535 S.W. Barnes Rd., #112, Portland, OR 97225. (Store hours are Monday, 10 A.M. to 5 P.M., and Tuesday through Saturday, 10 A.M. to 6 P.M., PST. They are closed on Sunday.)

HAPPY DOG BAKERY

Davenport, Iowa, is home to Happy Dog Bakery with "gourmutt treats and treasures." They have a wide variety of all-natural dog treats that contain no salt, sugar, artificial flavorings, or preservatives. The gourmutt treats, which come in different shapes, include Peanut Kitties, Pizza Bones, Honey Oat Bears, Beefy Bones, Bacon & Egg Piglets, Veggie Treats, Liver Lovers, Bark-B-Q-Ribs, Carol Biscotti, Lamb Dog Treat, Chicken 'N Stars, Dipped Doggy Donuts, and much more including special diet treats, gift baskets, and they even have cat treats for your dog's feline friends. And they have hypoallergenic and low-fat treats for dogs that need something special.

They offer gifts for dogs and their humans. Dog accessories include bowls, mats, and feeding stations. Human gifts include dog-themed doormats, breed sculptures, and more. Their website features an online tour of their store and information on how you can open your own Happy Dog Bakery. If you're in the neighborhood, you can visit the store with your dog but please be sure he's on leash. Your canine companion will receive a special treat.

For information: happydogbakery.com; e-mail: happydog@happy dogbakery.com; telephone (toll-free): 888-401-0990 (Phone orders are taken Monday through Friday, 10 A.M. to 5:30 P.M., and Saturday, 10 A.M. to 4 P.M.); fax: 309-764-1878; *Store locations:* Happy Dog Bakery, 1608 7th St., Moline, IL 62265 and 2218 East 11th St., Davenport, IA 52803.

HAWAII DOGGIE BAKERY & GIFT SHOP

This is Hawaii's original dog bakery and upscale boutique for dogs and their people and features the work of more than two hundred artists. Among the items sold are a Hawaiian cookbook for doggie delights and Aloha Bow-Wow Bone Dog Toys. Their website also lists the special events that take place in their shop. Dog Bakery treats include dog paw-ty specialties such as cakes and leis, Kalua Chicken and Poi Munchies, and Fish-n-Poi Pup Treats. They also carry seasonal items such as Beggin' Banana Poi Treats. Examples of the daily selections include Tail Waggin' Won Tons®, Doggie Dim Sum®, Loco Moco Biscuits, and Malu's Manapua. And if you want to know what any of this is, you'll either have to visit the store or the website. They even have Doggie Bento® like the local Bento Box lunches but filled with a selection of their doggie treats.

Every year, Hawaii Doggie Bakery & Gift Shop has an annual community service project called Pounds for Hounds. They give away more than three hundred pounds of free healthy Hawaiian doggie biscuits at dog parks around Hawaii. The treats are made with fresh local ingredients, making these treats unlike many others because they're based on a traditional Hawaiian diet. Some of the ingredients include taro, poi, and breadfruit. You can order by phone using their toll-free number. And you can join their mailing list to receive a monthly calendar that includes coupons, daily in-store specials, and more. The company is owned by two sisters, three Golden Retrievers, and two Labrador Retrievers. Hawaii Doggie Bakery & Gift Shop has three locations as well as an Internet site.

For information: hawaiidoggiebakery.com; e-mail: hawaiidoggie bakery@hawaii.rr.com; telephone (toll-free): 877-949-DOGS or (local): 808-949-DOGS. The main office and baking site is located at 2038 South King St., Honolulu, HI 96826. *Store locations:* Victoria Ward Centers, 1050 Ala Moana Blvd., Honolulu, HI (ground floor below the Spaghetti Factory); telephone: 808-521-PAWS. Pearlridge Center-Uptown, 98-1005 Moanalua Rd., Aiea, HI 96701; telephone: 808-487-PAWS.

HEALTH MUTTS

This company has healthy home-baked dog cookies as well as gift baskets for dogs and their human companions. In fact, they even do a sympathy basket to help cope with the loss of a beloved companion. Their dog treats are individually hand-rolled and cut, and they use the highest quality ingredients.

Their cookies have no preservatives, salt, or sugar. They are crunchy for your dog's enjoyment and reportedly smell delicious. The cookies come in a range of tastes and shapes, including Carrot Crunchers made like butterflies; Cheddar Cheezers, shaped like a hydrant; P-Nutters, shaped like a paw; and wheat-free Cheezers, shaped like a Terrier.

Health Mutts gift baskets are filled with dog treats and toys to delight the canine recipient. Gift mugs come complete with goodies for both dog and owner, including coffee for the owner and toys for the dog as well as treats for both. They also carry dog toys and gifts for the human companion. They offer an Outward Hound gift complete with an Outward Hound foldable bowl and a new dog or new puppy gift assortment that includes a stainless steel bowl with paw print and bone design on it.

Various retailers in California carry Health Mutts products, or you can order online. They also make dog party favors and doggie birthday cakes.

There's an online monthly photo contest at the Health Mutts website. You could win four bags of Health Mutts cookies for your canine companion.

In an effort to give back to the community, the owner donates any broken cookies to the no-kill shelter, Animal Rescue of Fresno, and she participates in the fund-raising activities of other shelters. She often donates gift baskets for silent auctions and fund-raising events in her area.

For information: healthmutts.com; e-mail: contact@healthmutts.com; telephone: 559-299-4320; fax: 559-298-4278; Health Mutts, 2318 E. Fallbrook Ave., Fresno, CA 93720.

H. O. FOOSE TINSMITHING—COOKIE CUTTERS

If you want to make your own dog cookies or cut cookies for humans into appealing canine-themed shapes for a party, meeting, dog-rescue group, or just for the family, you can find some very clever cookie cutters beyond the usual dog-bone shape. This family-owned business has been making cookie cutters by hand since the early 1970s. The stepdaughter of the company's founder now runs it.

They boast of more than seven hundred original cookie-cutter designs. Not all of them dogs, of course. Among the cookie-cutter shapes you can buy here are Corgi, Dachshund, the ubiquitous dog bone and paw shapes, German Shepherd, Greyhound, Poodle, Schnauzer, Scottie, a generic Terrier, and more.

While cookie cutters were originally made with full backs and handles, they are now backless and without handles. You can also find miniature cookie cutters that you could use to make hors d'oeuvres as well as cookies. The website also has ideas, recipes, and baking supplies but they encourage you to visit their store if you're in the area, since they have even more there than you will find on the Web. An interesting bit of company history: they once made a cookie cutter in the shape of a violin that was designed for Eugene Ormandy, the conductor of the Philadelphia Symphony Orchestra.

For information: foosecookiecutters.com; e-mail: sylvia@foosecookie cutters.com; telephone: 610-944-1961; fax: 610-944-6420; *Store location:* Foose Tinsmithing Company, 18 W. Poplar St., Fleetwood, PA 19522.

HOLISTIC DOG

Holistic Dog has all-natural gourmet dog treats and biscuits. They're baked fresh using the finest human-grade ingredients and they contain no wheat, corn, soy, salt, or sugar. Your dog can enjoy peanut treats and honey-baked treats, or you can purchase a bag of treat mix. They will not offer a product that they wouldn't use themselves.

They also carry other products for dogs, including copper cookie cutters, collars, and leashes. And, they carry diet supplements. They offer a 100 percent, money-back guarantee on everything they sell.

For information: holisticdog.com; e-mail: service@holisticdog.com; telephone (toll-free in United States): 800-595-1688 or (outside the United States): 541-282-7869 (Phone hours are Monday through Friday, 9 A.M. to 5 P.M., PST.); fax: 503-218-7701; Holistic Dog, 950 N. Phoenix Rd., Medford, OR 97504.

HOWLIN' MOON BAKERY

Howlin' Moon Bakery can be found on the Internet. They have an assortment of original homemade treats that are taste tested by the bakery owners' dog. The bakery is owned by a married couple—a Web developer, who loves to bake and loves her dog, and her husband, a graduate of the Culinary Institute of America in Hyde Park, New York. As of this writing, the bakery has three different original biscuits: Nutty

Banana Oats, Beef Stew, and the owners' dog's favorite, Howlin' Moon Chicken Parmesan. Biscuits are baked fresh daily, and the order usually goes out the day after it's received at the bakery. If not completely satisfied, you can return the remaining portion for a full refund.

Their website clearly states that while nutritious, the biscuits are treats and should be used accordingly. They recommend asking your veterinarian for the proper amount to give to your dog. Ingredients are listed on the package as well as on the website, so you can check for ingredients to which your dog might be allergic. They also sell bake-your-own biscuits ready mix, toy-and-treat combo packages, dog and cat beds, bandannas, and custom options for the beds and bandannas. Their website also has a monthly contest, a newsletter, and even a wish list.

For information: howlinmoonbakery.com; e-mail: treats@howlin moonbakery.com; telephone: 630-929-3688; Howlin' Moon Bakery, P.O. Box 246, Downers Grove, IL 60515.

HOWLING HOUND BAKERY

This doggy bakery boasts that their treats are low fat, organic, and "delicious." The business started because the owner's first dog, a pound puppy, had food allergies. Meatless dog treats were hard to find, so she created her own using vegetarian recipes. Not only did that dog love them but so did the second shelter dog acquired by the family.

Their treats contain no meat products or preservatives, and they come in mouthwatering names such as Peanut Butter Bones, Cheese Biscuits, Oatmeal Apples, Salsa Stars, Pizza Slices, Nutty Bananas, Very Berries, and Brownie Hearts (made with carob, not chocolate, of course). The bakery owner admits to eating the goodies herself, since they're made with human-grade ingredients. Gift packs are also available, as are gift certificates. She also wholesales to stores around the United States.

For information: howlinghound.com; e-mail: howlinghound@hotmail .com; telephone (toll-free): 888-323-HOWL; Howling Hound Bakery, P.O. Box 52225, Summerville, SC 29485.

K9 WATER CO.

This isn't just bottled water with a cute label, although the fact that their labels are cute doesn't hurt. Although they carry flavor names such as Toilet Water, Puddle Water, Hose Water, and Gutter Water, the bottles are filled with the world's first vitamin-fortified water specifically formulated for dogs, providing hydration and vitamins. They refer to it as Rebarkably Refreshing!™ The four flavors are, despite the funny names, chicken, beef, liver, and lamb. You can buy just one flavor or a four pack including each flavor. Only purified water and human-grade ingredients are used; no artificial colors or preservatives are added.

To make sure the water is healthy, the company's owners (dog owners themselves) had their formula tested by a veterinary nutritionist at an independent lab. The owners then had tasting parties for the four flavors. K9 Water Co., Inc., contributes to animal-rescue programs and the company's president is active in the ASPCA Advocacy Brigade, donates time to New Leash on Life Animal Rescue, and sponsors two adopted wolves at the Wolf Mountain Sanctuary in California. The company also sells K9 Water Co. T-shirts, sweatshirts, and a baby doll T-shirt.

They have a dog-of-the-month contest on their website. The FAQ section on the website is well worth reading and includes the product's testing information regarding safety/risk of toxicity.

The website (where you can purchase the water) features a chart that indicates how much of the vitamin-fortified water your dog can safely drink, which is determined by your dog's weight. It is formulated for dogs only, and they make no guarantees if you give it to another species. They do not recommend it for dogs with disease, and it's not formulated to aid in the treatment of specific ailments. They refer you to your veterinarian for expert advice.

They will accept returns of damaged, unopened bottles only for a full refund, exchange, or credit. K9 Wear that hasn't been worn or laundered may be exchanged only. All returns must be made within fourteen days.

For information: k9waterco.com; e-mail: info@k9waterco.com; telephone: 661-702-0211; K9 Water Co., Inc., 24332 Caladium Pl., Valencia, CA 91354.

LATKA'S DELICIOUS DOGGIE TREATS™

These all-natural doggie treats are baked under Latka's supervision. Latka, of course, is the owner's dog. He is an adorable Polish Lowland Sheepdog who was named after Latka Gravas, the character on the old TV series "Taxi." Latka's treats are made with freshly ground peanut butter using unsalted peanuts. All treats are handmade, using human-grade ingredients but without sugar, salt, colorings, preservatives, or additives. They continue to work to develop new flavors. You can purchase treat bags and boxes, a birthday basket that includes treats in a variety of shapes, and three bouncy balls for your canine friend's pleasure.

If you're planning a doggie birthday party, Latka's can create birthday bags for each guest with custom-printed labels on them saying Happy Birthday including your dog's name, a nifty little souvenir for the canine partygoers. They also have a teddy bear basket, a flower-power basket, and they have special holiday-themed baskets and tins during the year.

Latka's treats can be found at select stores including the New York Historical Society Museum Store. Contests are listed at the special promotions area of the website, as is a birthday club for your dog, dog tales, links, and more. And you can also find instructions on the website for keeping the treats fresh as well as a notice to check with your veterinarian before giving your dog any new food if she or he has allergies.

For information: delicioustreats.com; e-mail: latka@delicioustreats .com or (wholesale inquiries): wholesale@delicioustreats.com; Latka's Delicious Doggie Treats, P.O. Box 231384, Ansonia Station, New York, NY 10023.

MISS LILY'S BISCUITS™

Lily, the company's namesake, is a shelter dog who is now, according to their website, the CEO—chief eating officer. An assortment of biscuits and shapes are available including Happy Hearts and Razzle Dazzle Delights, which come in either orange or banana flavor. You can also find a pizza for dogs, Decadent Delight's carob biscuits in a choice of three flavors including crème de menthe, and bone-shaped biscuits half dipped in carob or yogurt (and some have sprinkles, too). Then there are Lily's Lovely Liver Snaps and more. The company even has Miss Lily's Shark Bites for your feline friend. All ingredients are listed on the website. You can also find an assortment of keepsake tins that you can use to keep the biscuits fresh. The company also sells K9 Water, premixed with vitamins specifically for dogs and flavored to appeal to them. Miss Lily's Biscuits also has a section on their website where you can see their upcoming event appearances.

Merchandise purchased can be returned to their distribution center within thirty days of purchase. Return instructions are on the packing slip. You will have to pay the return postage and insure them.

For information: misslilysbiscuits.com; e-mail is available from the website; telephone: 716-400-4698; Miss Lily's Biscuits, P.O. Box 215, North Boston, NY 14110.

OLD DOG COOKIE COMPANY

The all-natural dog treats sold by this company were created for pets who are either geriatric or have diabetes. The company was founded because the owner's dog, Drakes Island Jetty, had developed signs of arthritis. The arthritis relief cookies contain a variety of ingredients, including herbs, vitamins, minerals, and something the website refers to as "essential elements" to build strong joints and relieve inflammation. While this certainly isn't a prescription, every dog enjoys treats, which also include alfalfa and cod liver oil as well as vitamin C.

Jetty has Lyme disease and developed diabetes after that. By that time, having developed the arthritis cookies, his owner had begun making diabetic treats. These contain fiber and herbs as well as brewer's yeast. The company clearly states that the diabetic dog also requires regular veterinary care along with consistent exercise and optimum weight maintenance. The website provides a link to download or print out their brochure or flyer, or they will mail one to you at your request.

For information: olddogcookie.com; e-mail: info@olddogcookie.com; telephone (toll-free): 888-334-9DOG; Old Dog Cookie Company, Inc., 19 Island Beach Rd., Wells, ME 04090.

PAWPRINTS DOG PHOTO TREATS

Just when you think you've seen it all, along comes dog-photo treats. Like the photos on cakes for human family members, this company will help you put your dog's photo on a dog biscuit. All you have to do is choose your favorite photo and e-mail it as a .jpg file (150 DPI) to the company. The better the photo image, the better it will be on the cookies. They suggest that you avoid harsh lighting or photos that have shadows or are poorly focused. You can specify which area of the photo you want reproduced on the cookies, otherwise, they will crop for what the company feels is the best image. If you prefer, you can send your photo via regular mail. Just print out the order form from the website and send the photo with your order. Be sure to put your name and address on the back of the photo because it will be returned with your order. And write "do not bend" on the envelope. Better yet, use a special photo envelope or line a regular envelope with cardboard to prevent bending. It takes about a week for your order to arrive.

Essentially, you will receive a kit with the cookies. The kit contains premade cookies (the top layer looks like a frame) and a sheet of edible pictures. You will then create a doggie sandwich cookie using special treats as filling. The company suggests dog toothpaste for a healthy treat, but you can also use tuna, cream cheese, peanut butter, or the dog's favorite canned food. The kit includes edible images of your dog, sets of doggie cookies, and easy to follow illustrated instructions.

The cookies are freshly baked, made with highest quality, all-natural ingredients: whole-wheat flour, eggs, water, peanut oil, and non-fat dried skim milk. The images are printed with food colors on potato paper. The cookies are vacuum packed and will stay fresh about a month in the packaging, longer if refrigerated. When the package arrives all you'll have to do is unwrap the cookies, spread the filling, and add your dog's image and cookie on top. The website is careful to say that you should consult your veterinarian before using the cookies, always good advice when giving a new food or treat.

For information: dogphototreats.com; e-mail: yummy@dogphoto treats.com; Jake Bakes, Pawprint Dog Photo Treats, Inc., PMB 670, 8168 W. McNab Rd., North Lauderdale, FL 33068.

THE PET BAKERY

This family-owned pet bakery and boutique features doggie goodies such as biscotti half dipped in carob or yogurt, Thumb Print Ginger Morsels with yogurt cream, Peanut Butter Goober, Thumbs Up Cheese Twist, and Bow Wow Ginger Snaps. The bakery owner also owns a pet-sitting service, Petwatch, Inc., in Palm Beach County, Florida.

They have holiday parties at the store for virtually every occasion. Dogs are invited, of course, and some come dressed for the holiday. A visit to their website will show you photos from Valentine's Day and Easter.

For information: thepetbakery.com; info@thepetbakery.com; telephone: 561-649-4364; fax: 561-649-5952. *Store location:* The Pet Bakery Lantana Square Shopping Center, 6169 Jog Rd., Suite C11-A, Lake Worth, FL 33467.

PIGLET'S PANTRY DOG BAKERY

Yes, that's right. Piglet's Pantry, located in Mount Dora, Florida, is a dog bakery, named for the owner's rescued racing Greyhound. Piglet is now living a life of leisure with devoted owners. He serves as the official taste tester for all the doggie goodies baked at Piglet's Pantry. The cookies are made without sugar, salt, or preservatives. Baked items include Bubba Q's; Buddy Ohs; Carob Bonz; Carob Lovers Tray; Charcoal Bonz; Charcoal Sticks; Chicken & Rice Bonz; Double Dipped Bone; Happy Birthday Sack of Treats; Healthy Bones in various varieties including apple, banana, fish and potato, and more; Kricket Krunchies in such flavors as fresh blueberries and cranberries; and Honey Granola; MoonDog Bonz; Peanut Butter Bonz; and you can even get Piglet's Biscuit Mix and do it yourself at home. You can also find Piglet's Pizza and more, including variety packs or their products. All ingredients are listed at the website if you're ordering online.

The website includes links to rescue dogs along with gift items, including afghans in various dog breeds, a bone doorbell, and more. Check for "specials" on the baked goodies. Look for a fun section of "mind games" that dogs can play with their owners, in addition to a news section. Piglet's Pantry also welcomes inquiries for wholesaling their baked goods.

For information: pigletspantry.com; telephone (toll-free): 888-Piglet4 or (local): 352-735-9779; Piglet's Pantry, Inc., Dog Bakery, 400 N. Donnelly St., Mount Dora, FL 32757.

PINK BELLY ICE PUPS™

Pink Belly Ice Pups are billed as cool treats for dogs. They're all-natural and preservative free, with no added sugar or salt, and come in a variety of flavors including Paw Berry, Bone'illa, Chubby Puppy, Monkey Madness, Four Leaf Rover, and Peppermint Patty. Ingredients for the flavors are listed at the website and include special seasonal ones like Pupkin during Thanksgiving and Christmas. They have retired flavors, but some do return like Cocka-Poodle-Do. The Ice Pups' main ingredient is yogurt, to which wholesome foods are added for flavor. A portion of the profits is donated to humane societies.

The Pink Belly Ice Pups are sold at dog cafés, doggie day cares, and pet boutiques, as well as at the company's website. The company's corporate mission is to decrease the country's pound population. They are also happy to be contacted by anyone looking for veterinarians, dog walkers, adoption centers, groomers, and so forth in the Boca Raton, Florida, area. If you or your dog would like to contact Lucy, the little Yorkie who inspired the business, you can e-mail her at her very own e-mail account. Check out Lucy's very own page on the website. *For information:* pinkbelly.com; e-mail: belly@pinkbelly.com or (Lucy): lucy@pinkbelly.com; telephone: 561-376-5990. Pink Belly, Inc., 4005 Village Dr., Suite B, Delray Beach, FL 33445.

REBA'S HEALTHY GOURMET DOGGY COOKIES

Reba's Dog Cookies are made in Clatskanie, Oregon, and named for the owner's dog. The cookies are homemade, hand-rolled, hand-cut, and preservative free. The crunchy cookies are made with only fresh, all-natural, human-grade ingredients. The basic recipe contains four vegetables, one fruit, and depending upon the chosen flavor, more vegetables, fruit, meat, cheese, and fish. They also add brewer's yeast, a vitamin and mineral supplement, and garlic. They do not add salt, fat, sugar, or coloring. A touch of pure honey is added to some of the flavors. Farm-fresh eggs are used as are fresh garlic and organic raspberries and mint, and freshly ground peanut butter. The cookies come in eleven flavors, including venison, mint and honey, beef liver, and broccoli and cheese. They feature a flavor of the month, such as pumpkin spice, a special of the month, seasonal shaped cookies for holidays, and you can custom order special-occasion or holiday gift baskets, puppy treats, obedience-training nuggets, tiny bones for small dogs, super bones for big dogs, wheat- and corn-free cookies, and there's Reba's Cookie Club. They offer a money-back guarantee on all orders. If you're not completely satisfied, you can return the item within fourteen days and it will either be replaced or your money will be returned (less the shipping costs)—the choice is yours.

For information: http://awesomedogtreats.safeshopper.com; e-mail: dazzle@clatskanie.com; telephone: 508-728-4664 or 508-369-2171; Reba's Dog Cookies, 21740 Lindberg Rd., Clatskanie, OR 97016.

TAIL WAGGIN' BAKERY (SEA4YOURSELF, INC.)

From dog biscuits to barking cookie jars, you'll find it at Tail Waggin' Bakery. Their biscuits include delights such as Yum Yum Cones, Bark-a-Cino, Sheltie Smores, and Carob Blossoms. They also make specialty cookies that are carob filled, dipped, or chipped, and/or topped with yogurt. They come in several shapes and varieties. The bakery also makes birthday cakes and cookies as well as Barking Bagels and Bone Cookies. They have bagged treats and they make gift baskets. They also offer specialty gifts.

The website has features such as a list of toxic plants, and you can also consult a recipe page that includes treats such as Shih Tzu Sushi, Schnauzer Sausage, Muttloaf, and much, much more. You can join their mailing list as well as sign your companion up for the birthday club. Pets who are members of the birthday club receive treats via the mail in honor of their special day. Check out a separate section on the website with goodies for cats.

If you're in the Toledo, Ohio, area you can visit their bakery and see the full array of yummy treats.

For information: sea4yourself.bigstep.com; e-mail is available from the website; telephone: 419-351-9463; fax: 419-885-1747. *Store location:* Tail Waggin' Bakery, 237 S. Erie St., Toledo, OH 43602.

THREE DOG BAKERY

Likely the largest chain of bake shops for dogs (they have shops in Canada as well as the United States), Three Dog Bakery began operation in 1989. The brainchild of Dan Dye and Mark Beckloff, they adore their three dogs and wanted to offer them fresh-baked dog biscuits without all of the additives. After consulting veterinarians, they opened their first store, creating recipes with the help their own and their neighbors' four-legged taste testers. They now have many stores throughout the United States and they have a mail-order business through their website. Along with biscuits, they offer celebration cakes and monthly "dogliveries."

They founded and continue to support The Gracie Foundation, which was named for one of their original three dogs. They describe it as being like a "canine Red Cross." The foundation offers financial support to any properly licensed, not-for-profit companion-animal group that focuses on rescue and is not receiving any tax support. Their informative website will also allow you to search out their stores.
For information: threedogbakery.com; e-mail: threedog@threedog .com; telephone (toll-free): 800-4-TREATS (Phone hours are Monday through Friday, 8 A.M. to 5 P.M., CST.); fax: 816-474-2171; Three Dog Bakery, 1627 Main St., Suite 700, Kansas City, MO 64108.

TULIP'S DOG & CAT BAKERY

Riverside, California, is home to Tulip's Dog & Cat Bakery where homemade, all-natural treats are the order of the day. Treats for dogs include Maggie's Beagle Bagels, Eddie's Barking Bones, After Dinner Mints, Ginger Hearts, Max's Muffinetts, Patch's Cinnamon & Carrot Pupcakes, Tulip's Peanut Butter Pups, Molasses Paws, Peanut Butter Terriers, and more. In case you're wondering, the bakery is named for the owner's English Bulldog, Tulip. The family also includes a Yellow Lab–German Shepherd mix and a cat. There's another English Bulldog in the extended family. Tulip's Dog & Cat Bakery is a home-based business. They attend fairs, market events, and festivals, and you can order online. They ship nationwide in the United States.
For information: tulipsbakery.com; e-mail: stephanie@tulipsbakery .com; telephone: 909-777-0104.

INTERNATIONAL

BIG DOG LITTLE DOG BAKERY

The owners say that this is where your dog's dreams come true. They make their treats using fresh ingredients with no added salt, sugar, coloring, or preservatives. They are also careful to ensure that their treats are appealingly tasty to the dog. They make a variety of items in a wide range of flavors. Among the more than a dozen crunchy treats are Liver Slivers, Veggie Strong Bones, Wishy Fishy Bones (made with salmon), Scare-dee Cats, and Peanut Butter Bis-Scotties. Squares include Tuna Squares and Liver Squares. Big cookie flavors include Cheesy Bears, Ginger Guys, and Vanilla Cranberry Flowers. Deli items include Turkey Meatballs, Bison Bones, Musk-Ox Bones, and Chicken Sausage Rolls. Dipped cookies include Oats and P.B. Bones, Drizzled Bones, and their 10-Inch Monster Bones can be personalized. They also do an assortment of cakes and specialty items, including Pup-Cakes and Carob Truffle. The company also carries gifts, accessories, and more. They have specials and promotions, which you can find online or at their store. Their products are found not just on the Web, but in their own store and at pet supply stores in various places in British Columbia. The list of locations can be found on the website.

For information: bigdoglittledog.com; e-mail: info@bigdoglittledog .com; telephone: 604-299-DOG; fax: 604-299-3655. *Store location:* Big Dog Little Dog Bakery, 4631 Hastings St., Burnaby, BC, V5C 2K6, Canada. (Store hours are Tuesday through Sunday, 10 A.M. to 6 P.M.)

CHATFIELD DOG CAKES

Yes, cakes for dogs, baked individually to your dog's delight. The cakes are homemade and hand finished, and each looks like a rich fruitcake. However, they are full of ingredients your dog will enjoy and come in three different flavors. The liver and carrot cake contains organic carrot, lamb's liver, stout, and garlic. The bacon and cheese cake contains free-range bacon and Stilton cheese. The three cheeses cake is a mixture of Stilton, cheddar, and Parmesan. The bacon and cheese and three cheeses cakes contain a yeast extract. All eggs used to make the cakes come from free-range chickens.

Each cake comes with a personalized gift tag and is wrapped with a ribbon and silk flower. This makes a lovely gift for the dog who has everything. The cakes are available in two sizes: 5 inches (12.5 centimeters) or 6 inches (15 centimeters) in diameter. A cake mix is coming for those who want to bake their own dog cakes. You'll find two order forms at the website; one is for orders in the United Kingdom and the other is for orders from the European Union countries. To purchase their products outside of Europe, please query. Postage is included in the price.

For information: dogcakes.co.uk; e-mail: info@dogcakes.co.uk; telephone: 0114 2331486; Jane Chatfield, Chatfield Dog Cakes, 8 Robertson Rd., Sheffield, South Yorkshire S6 5DX, United Kingdom.

4

Read All About It

You'll find a plethora of material written for dog owners. Some of it is good, but some is bad. It's important to know how to separate the wheat from the chaff so you can make an informed decision when spending your hard-earned money on a book or magazine. Be certain that what you buy reflects a dog-care philosophy with which you agree, not something that merely rehashes outmoded ideas, especially when it comes to teaching your dog manners. Most people have replaced the old jerk-and-yank methods with positive training. Some dog trainers are still using old methods, while others have moved along the continuum and progressed to newer training methodologies, such as operant conditioning. The teaching books getting the lion's share of publicity might not be the ones you want. You must decide for yourself. Select materials that reflect your own philosophy, but also be open to publications that present new and fresh ideas that aren't rehashed by a writer looking to raise his or her profile. As with so many other purchases, caveat emptor: let the buyer beware.

Everyone is somewhere on the continuum. You will want to move forward with training books that advance positive methods, and if you have a purebred dog, you'll want at least one good breed book in your collection to create a useful library. The books you buy will be ones you'll read and reread. And you may find yourself tearing articles out of magazines and keeping them on file.

BOOKS

While a number of Internet outlets sell dog books, including online bookstores, you can find shops dedicated solely to dog books.

DOG LOVERS BOOKSHOP

Once a bookstore in Manhattan, this is now strictly an online business. They now specialize in hard-to-find used, out-of-print, and rare books although they have a small selection of new books. Their emphasis is on small presses as well as university press books. They carry books not only about dogs, but wolves, coyotes, foxes, dingoes, and wild dogs. Most books are in English but many are in other languages. They also have illustrated children's books. And, they have a selection of videotapes.

The website is updated each week and has a detailed table of contents with a guide that explains how books are categorized and chosen, and it defines the terms and abbreviations used on the site. The owners have written their own book for book collectors, *Care and Feeding of Books Old and New*.

They ship books around the world, and they're happy to help if you need advice or perhaps want more details about a specific book. They also buy books.

For information: dogbooks.com; e-mail: info@dogbooks.com; telephone and fax: 212-369-7554; Dog Lovers Bookshop, P.O. Box 117, Gracie Station, New York, NY 10028.

DOGREAD LIST

In the western part of the United States, Drs. Treshell and Tomas Jones got the idea for this list when they realized they had a pile of dog books waiting to be read. They realized that others must also collect and enjoy dog books but don't have much time to read. Thus began one of the best ideas on the Internet.

In March 2000, they started a list with twenty-three people. As word spread, it quickly grew to nearly four thousand subscribers internationally. The list serves as a monthly seminar and a cyber book club in workshop format with some well-known names in the dog world, many of whom lecture around the United States and internationally. Each month everyone reads the same dog book at the same time. Best of all, the author is on the list for the entire month and list members can ask questions. The list is usually closed on the weekends so list members can "go out and play with their dogs." All of the posts are kept archived, so new list members, as well as long-standing ones, can go back through them and read any months they might have missed.

The list owners have arranged for three online companies to offer a special discount on books to list members: Dogwise, SitStay, and NCConcepts. Among the authors who have appeared on DogRead are such notables as Turid Rugaas, Morgan Spector, Karen Pryor, Pat Hastings, George Alston, and Jean Donaldson. The list owners sponsor a special award for "Best Book" through the Dog Writers Association of America. The author of DWAA's best book of the year receives, along with their DWAA Maxwell Award, a plaque, a check, and a month as guest speaker on the DogRead list.

For information: dogread.com. To subscribe, send a blank e-mail to dogread-subscribe@yahoogroups.com.

DOGWISE

If you're a book-a-holic and a dog lover, you'll want to check out Dogwise. This online bookstore is devoted to dog books, videos, games, and a few training items (clickers, target sticks, and so forth). Their online bookstore allows you to write reader reviews. They also have message boards, with authors responding to questions at various times. They also have a booth that travels to dog shows. Their warehouse is open to the public, who can take a basket and grab books just as the employees would when filling an order. It's not unusual for customers to stagger out under an armload of books. Dogwise also publishes dog books. *For information:* dogwise.com; telephone for phone orders (toll-free): 800-776-2665. **Warehouse location:** Dogwise, 701 B. Poplar, Wenatchee, WA 98801.

4-M DOG BOOKS

4-M Dog Books (4-M Enterprises) can be found online as well as at dog shows. "If we don't have it, we'll do our doggonedest to get it for you," is not just the company's slogan; it's their way of life. They strive to have in-print, out-of-print, and rare books available. They also carry calendars and videos.

For information: 4mdogbooks.com; e-mail: info@4mdogbooks.com; telephone (toll-free): 800-487-9867; 4-M Enterprises, Inc., Everything in Dog Books, 34937 Peco St., Union City, CA 94587.

INTERNATIONAL

BOOKWORLD INTERNATIONAL

If you live in the United Kingdom, or want to order books from there that aren't available in the United States, Bookworld International is a good source. They are on the Internet and they travel to various dog shows and agricultural events. Owned by Robin and Diana Sadler, who are dog breeders as well as International Championship show judges who specialize in Gundogs (sporting breeds) and Hounds, they refer to their business as a specialist dog book company covering all aspects of sensible dog ownership.

For information: dogbooks.co.uk or (for their reviews of new books): dogbookreviews.com; telephone and fax: 44 (0) 1544 230794; Highfield, Walton Green, Presteigne, Powys LD8 2PU, Wales, United Kingdom.

CROSSKEYS BOOKS

Crosskeys Books is an online bookstore and publisher in England that specializes in books about positive training, specifically, operant conditioning (clicker training). They are also part of a three-acre site with a store, an education center, a training and behavior center, and boarding kennels. People often stop by to read, observe, and talk about books. Visitors can, of course, purchase books on site. A forty-eight-page color brochure of their mail-order products is available free of charge from any of Crosskeys' four websites.

Owner Stephen G. King sells his own books along with those of others such as Karen Pryor. He also offers videotapes by Professor Ray Coppinger and Nina Bondarenko. Also featured are veterinary behavior texts by Dr. Bonnie Beaver and Dr. Karen Overall and much more.

The websites have far more on them than pet behavior and training books, although that's their specialty. They are full of resources for pet owners with links to such topics as grooming, kennels, rescue, and a variety of training topics including agility, heelwork to music, and scent training. Crosskeys also sells videos and pet products. They also sell Stephen G. King's clicker cue cards that help solve six problem behaviors. You can find book reviews at the site and you can submit your own reviews. The website has a members section that you can join free of charge. It will allow you access to more features including articles by such people as Attila Szkukalek, Ph.D., Eddie Fernandez, B.Sc., and more. There is also a special offer of the month at a special members discounted price. You can subscribe to a newsletter or check the section listing events.

For information: crosskeysbooks.com, crosskeyspetproducts.co.uk, clickerzoneuk.co.uk, or havaball.co.uk; e-mail: info@crosskeysbooks .com; telephone: 020 8590 3604; fax: 020 8599 6177; Crosskeys Select Books, Collier Row Rd., Romford, Essex, RM5 2BH, United Kingdom.

NK CONCEPTS

NK Concepts in Canada has books, videos, training supplies and equipment, toys, hard-to-find dog obedience objects, and more. They are an online bookstore with a presence at some dog shows. Their dog books cover all aspects of dog ownership and care from breed books to training, behavior, and more.

It's worth spending some time exploring their website and checking out the many features, including a listing of upcoming dog events in Canada; or the Toy Box for the latest scoop on dog toys; and the Trading Post, which has things to trade, sell, or buy. You can read news updates from Michelle Armitage, a CKC-licensed obedience judge who writes about her dogs and her training; Tiffany Salmon from agility and flyball, who reports on her Border Collies, Piper and Rio; Doug

Bender and Hunter, with reports on conformation; Rita Susanto gives the latest news from the obedience ring; and "Behavior Bites," with Robin Rosay. And you can also read news from others in the world of obedience. New people and their dogs are expected to be added to the list of reporters.

NK Concepts is an online dog supply company, specializing in finding and ordering hard-to-find supplies for dogs and various types of dog sports such as obedience, agility, and freestyle. NK Concepts can also be found at dog shows in Ontario and Quebec. And their website is available in French as well as English.

For information: nkconcepts.com; e-mail: nkitch@videotron.ca; telephone: 450-458-3165; fax: 450-458-3210 (please call main number before faxing); NK Concepts–Dog Supplies, 156 Fair Haven, Hudson, QC, J0P 1H0, Canada.

MAGAZINES, NEWSLETTERS, AND NEWSPAPERS

A range of magazines, newsletters, and newspapers are devoted to dogs and their owners. They cover a wide range of topics for owners interested in everything from travel and fashion to those who are involved in dog sports or conformation dog shows. These publications provide articles on health, training, and handling as well as profiles of well-known individuals in the dog fancy.

AKC GAZETTE

The *AKC Gazette* is a magazine, the voice of the American Kennel Club. It contains articles and columns that are of interest mainly to those who breed and show dogs. However, they do have articles that appeal to pet owners as well, and breed columns rotate each month. They also profile a featured breed nearly every month. They publish articles on health, training, showing, behavior, and occasionally art, collectibles, and other topics of interest to dog owners. Available by subscription and on some newsstands, the *Gazette* subscription comes with the events calendar each month, listing shows and judging panels. The AKC also publishes *The Family Dog* magazine for pet owners.

For information: akc.org/pubs; e-mail (subscriptions): agzt@kable
.com; telephone (toll-free): 800-533-7323 or (toll-free for subscriptions to *The Family Dog*): 800-490-5675; *AKC Gazette*, Subscription
Service Dept., P.O. Box 1956, Marion, OH 43306-4056.

ANIMAL FAIR

Animal Fair calls itself the lifestyle magazine for animal lovers, and it
certainly lives up to that claim. It has real appeal to dog owners with
its glossy pages and interesting articles, many of which can be found
on their website as well. Regular features include "Reel Pets," which is
centered on entertainment; whether it's animals or celebrities from
films, television, music, and comedy, you'll find them here. They also
feature fashion shoots with humans as well as canine and feline models.
They also offer travel, fashion, beauty, design, and events sections, all
with an animal slant. "*AF* Cares" is a section on animal-related humane
organizations. They also have features on wildlife and petpourri. *Animal Fair* is available by subscription or online, or you can find it on
newsstands or at Barnes and Noble, Borders, Petco, and PETsMART.
For information: animalfair.com; e-mail: info@animalfair.com or subs
@animalfair.com; telephone: 212-629-0392 ext. 202; fax subscription
orders to: 212-629-0393; *Animal Fair* Subscriptions, P.O. Box 966,
New York, NY 10018.

THE BARK

Proclaiming "The Bark Unleashed," *The Bark* calls itself the voice of
modern dog culture. It certainly is different from other dog publications. This quarterly magazine has an aura of being more erudite. Its
pages are filled with stories, artwork, poetry, reviews, social and behavior issues, interviews, health, recreation, and activism. Yes, the same
blend you see in other magazines but this one has a decidedly different voice. While it focuses on dogs and their humans, it does it in a far
more sophisticated manner. Their website has activism and events
listed in the Community area.

The magazine is also quite entertaining and publishes commentaries and essays, fiction as well as nonfiction, how-to articles, and tips.
A sampling of articles appears on their website.

A one-year subscription includes five issues; a two-year subscription includes ten issues; you get fifteen issues in a three-year subscription. The magazine is also available in select locations. While being well known for its content, *The Bark* is also known for its slogan, "Dog is my co-pilot," which appears on T-shirts, sweatshirts, and bumper stickers, which are available at the website. The items can also be combined with a subscription.

For information: thebark.com; e-mail: bark@thebark.com; telephone (toll-free): 877-BarkNews or (local): 510-704-0827; fax: 510-704-0933; *The Bark*, 2810 8th St., Berkeley, CA 94710.

BLOODLINES

Bloodlines is the magazine of the United Kennel Club (UKC), which is the second-largest dog registry in the United States. (Only AKC is larger.) The UKC is also involved in supporting dog sports as well as conformation. *Bloodlines* contains articles on a variety of topics important to dog fanciers, including health, nutrition, handling, and grooming as well as show wins in UKC conformation, obedience, and agility trials. They feature breed articles, book reviews, and profiles of people in the dog community. *Bloodlines* is published monthly. Visa and Master Card customers can call the number that follows to subscribe.

For information: ukcdogs.com (click on "Publications"); telephone: 269-343-9020; *Bloodlines*, 100 East Kilgore Rd., Kalamazoo, MI 49002-5584.

CANINE CHRONICLE®

Canine Chronicle is the oldest, continually published, show-dog magazine in the United States and reputedly has the largest circulation of any show-dog magazine. Published monthly, it features full-page show-win advertisements, many of them in color, with their print quality comparable to *Architectural Digest*. The magazine also includes all-breed statistics, photographic essays on dog shows, as well as feature articles. It is decidedly for the show-dog aficionado. Their website has additional information that the pet owner would appreciate.

Canine Chronicle's website includes an online community that is a marvelous resource of links that will appeal to any dog owner, not just

those in the dog fancy. Not only are there links to AKC, CKC, The
Kennel Club, Japan KC, and FCI, but there's a list of dog seminars;
other links include dog-show superintendents; travel information
(including weather forecasts) for people off to dog shows; dog supplies;
breed rescue; and, most importantly, links to every veterinary school
in the United States so dog owners can get accurate veterinary information. That alone makes it worth surfing over to *Canine Chronicle*'s
website.

For information: caninechronicle.com; e-mail: k9chron@aol.com; fax:
352-369-1108; *The Canine Chronicle*, 4727 N.W. 80th Ave., Ocala, FL
34482.

DOG & HANDLER

Dog & Handler's mission statement says that the magazine is "dedicated to covering recreational and competitive sports in which all dogs,
regardless of pedigree, are welcome to participate." *Dog & Handler*'s
goal is to enlighten, inspire, and entertain handlers. They aim to appeal
to owners interested in a variety of dog-related topics and those at various levels of dog sports. "Content is limited to sports and other organized canine activities that involve positive, motivational, and
reward-based training methods." The magazine's goal is to advance
training and solidify the dog-owner bond. Lofty goals, indeed.

Dog & Handler covers all dog sports. You can sample the magazine
online with articles and contests, and you can see what readers have
said about the magazine that covers agility, flyball, herding, freestyle,
obedience, canine disc, event coverage, and more. You can also find
articles on recreational sports like skijoring, bikejoring, and hiking
with your dog, as well as articles of general interest to dog owners as
well as a calendar of events. You can subscribe online or via mail.

For information: dogandhandler.com; e-mail: info@dogandhandler
.com; telephone: 802-254-1209; *Dog & Handler*, 234 Butternut Hill
Rd., Guilford, VT 05301.

DOG & KENNEL

Dog & Kennel magazine publishes six issues per year and has a variety
of articles for pet owners, including topics such as veterinary medicine,

breed profiles, stories about dogs at work, as well as canine sports and stories about canines. Their online site gives you a taste of the magazine and has a message board as well as reader stories. You can also opt for a free trial issue subscription.

For information: dogandkennel.com; e-mail: dksubscriptions@pet publishing.com; telephone: 336-292-4047; fax: 336-292-4272; Pet Publishing, Inc., 7-L Dundas Cr., Greensboro, NC 27407.

DOG FANCY

Dog Fancy is primarily a magazine for pet owners. The magazine covers a wide range of topics pertaining to dogs, from breed profiles to training, health, and more. The newest issue can always be previewed on *Dog Fancy*'s website where they also have message boards and classified ads. As with all Fancy Publications, people who have animals for sale advertise. This does not imply an endorsement of these dogs or their breeders by the publication. It is up to the individual to do their research before buying a dog or puppy from anyone. The website has an online poll, and you can subscribe to the monthly publication while you're online. The magazines from Fancy Publications and their Bow Tie Press books are widely available.

For information: dogfancy.com; e-mail (for subscriptions): fancy@neo data.com; telephone (toll-free for subscriptions): 800-365-4421; Fancy Publications, 3 Burroughs, Irvine, CA 92618 or (for subscriptions) Dog Fancy Subscription Department, P.O. Box 53264, Boulder, CO 80322-3264.

DOG NEWS

Dog News is America's oldest weekly dog magazine. Dedicated to the dog show aficionado, *Dog News* features articles; regular columns, including veterinary topics and even a regular gossip column; as well as ads of show wins. It contains a directory of professional dog handlers and other information of interest to those involved in the sport of dogs. The *Dog News* top-ten list is a monthly listing of the top-ten dogs in each group, as well as within each breed. The list is based on group/all-breed competition and is updated on their website the Tuesday after the list runs in the weekly newspaper. The website contains a good deal of information and also makes some articles available online. A year's subscription includes fifty issues. You can subscribe online or via regular mail.

For information: dognews.com; e-mail: thedognews@aol.com; *Dog News*, 1115 Broadway, New York, NY 10010.

DOG WATCH®

Dog Watch is the newsletter from Cornell University specifically for dog people. It is published off-site, but the writers tap into the specialists at Cornell's veterinary school and small animal hospital when writing about a variety of topics of concern to dog owners including behavior, health, and nutrition. To subscribe, call their toll-free number or write to them at the address that follows.

For information: vet.cornell.edu/publicresources/dog.htm; telephone (toll-free): 800-829-5574; *Dog Watch*, P.O. Box 42035, Palm Coast, FL 32142-0235.

DOG WORLD

Dog World's subtitle is *The Authority on Dog Care*. This monthly magazine has a variety of articles including monthly "Meet the Breed" articles. They cover a wide range of topics including health, nutrition, training, and more. The magazine has been purchased by Fancy Publications. It is available on newsstands and by subscription.

For information: dogworldmag.com; e-mail (for editorial): dogworld @fancypubs.com or (for subscriptions): fancy@neodata.com (include "Dog World" in the subject line); telephone (toll-free for subscriptions): 800-365-4421 or (local): 949-855-8822; fax: 949-855-3045 or (for subscriptions): 641-842-6101; *Dog World* Magazine, P.O. Box 6050, Mission Viejo, CA 92690-6050 or (for subscriptions) Subscription Service Department, *Dog World*, P.O. Box 56244, Boulder, CO 80322-6244.

DOGS IN REVIEW

Dogs in Review calls itself "the magazine that matters." While it is geared to the dog-show community, unlike other magazines aimed at that audience, this magazine emphasizes editorial content—with in-depth articles written by specialists in their respective areas—as well as advertising. Launched in 1997, *Dogs in Review* is a monthly publication printed on glossy paper, which gives it an elegant look. *Dogs in Review* features bylines by notables in the fancy such as Anne Rogers Clark and Ron Menaker along with international canine journalists like Clive Davies; the magazine also has health features by Debra Eldredge, D.V.M., who is also active in the fancy. Editor Bo Bengtson was also the publisher until selling it to Fancy Publications. He remains as editor. You can subscribe online or via post.

For information: dogsinreview.com; e-mail: info@dogsinreview .com; telephone: 949-855-8822; fax: 949-855-1850; subscriptions, renewals, and all correspondence about subscriptions to *Dogs in Review*, P.O. Box 6040, Mission Viejo, CA 92690-6040; editorial address is P.O. Box 558, Creston, CA 93432.

FRONT AND FINISH®

Front and Finish is a monthly magazine for people who participate with their dogs in a variety of dog sports including obedience, agility, freestyle, flyball, field trials, herding, rally, and tracking. Their updated website allows subscribers to read issues online as well as in print. *Front and Finish* calls itself "an organization devoted to sport of amateur dog training and associated performance events." Their monthly magazine covers regional and national canine activities. They also sponsor educational events and they recognize exhibitors with a rating system and awards. Clubs and schools use their rating system to offer awards and honors to their members.

For information: frontandfinish.com or canineperformance.com; e-mail: mailbox@frontandfinish.com; telephone: 309-344-1333; *Front and Finish*, H. and S. Publications, Inc., R.T. Self, 2310 US Hwy. 150 N., Wataga, IL 61488.

LAUGHING DOG PRESS

There are seemingly countless dog-oriented websites: breed websites, dog-activity websites, and those dedicated to virtually any dog-related topic imaginable. They all have one thing in common: they're serious. Those who love dogs seem to share a wonderful sense of humor. The online magazine *Laughing Dog Press* recognizes this and fills that void. This site parodies everything from dog breeds to dog sports. It's all done in good fun by people who genuinely love dogs. If you're planning to surf over to this website, bring your sense of humor. Each month, *Laughing Dog Press* looks at a different breed from an off-beat, humorous angle.

They take the same lighthearted approach to dog sports. The *Laughing Dog* will share a distinctive view and will also answer questions from that unique perspective.

The website also has a store where you can find T-shirts and golf shirts with not only The *Laughing Dog Press* logo on them, but others with breed cartoons and humorous illustrations of dog sports like flyball and agility. They also feature an online contest. Enter an original cartoon, illustration, or piece of writing limited to five hundred words and you could win a free *Laughing Dog* T-shirt if you make the laughing dog chuckle. If you make him laugh he will publish your work and send you $50. There is also a free newsletter.

For information: laughingdogpress.com; e-mail: info@laughingdog press.com; Laughing Dog Press, P.O. Box 2276, Windsor, CA 95492.

OFF-LEAD & NATURAL PET

Off-Lead & Natural Pet, as the title implies, is a magazine about dog training and features a variety of training articles from all sorts of trainers, some of them quite positive like Morgan Spector, as well as features on dog sports like freestyle and those involved. Available by subscription, *Off-Lead* is published six times a year. It's geared to professional trainers and serious dog-training hobbyists, exhibitors, instructors, and behavior therapists as well as groomers, kennel operators, and pet care professionals.

For information: off-lead.com; e-mail: barkleigh@aol.com; telephone: 717-691-3388; fax: 717-691-3381; *Off-Lead*, 6 State Road, #113, Mechanicsburg, PA 17050.

SHOWSIGHT

ShowSight magazine is one of several published by Doll-McGinnis Publications and interests people who have any breed of purebred dog.

Doll-McGinnis's other publications include *The Orient Express*, *Top Notch Toys* (this is their only other magazine covering more than one breed), and *The Pom Reader*. *ShowSight* is a monthly magazine for those who enjoy participating in dog shows. It contains articles as well as show-win advertisements from those who show their dogs.

For information: dmcg.com; e-mail: jmcg@dmcg.com; telephone: 863-858-3839; Doll-McGinnis Publications, 8848 Beverly Hills, Lakeland, FL 33809-1604.

URBAN DOG MAGAZINE

The magazine's website states that "*Urban Dog Magazine* chronicles our love affair with our canine companions." This is a quarterly, regional magazine whose articles have appeal well beyond the borders of their distribution area. The articles are human-interest stories about dogs and their people. The stories are true and speak to everyone who loves dogs. At this writing, plans are in place to distribute the magazine beyond the current eighteen states where it's distributed.

The website has archived issues so you can read a sampling of articles, find a list of places where you can buy *Urban Dog*, and take the opportunity to subscribe. They have a shopping area that includes Guatemalan weave collars and matching leads, postcards, tags, charms, and T-shirts.

For information: urbandogmagazine.com; e-mail: sit@urbandog magazine.com; telephone: 504-897-9577; *Urban Dog Magazine*, 5500 Prytania St., #419, New Orleans, LA 70115.

WHOLE DOG JOURNAL

The *Whole Dog Journal* is a newsletter whose articles cover all aspects of dog care and training. Their emphasis is on natural care and complementary therapies, such as acupuncture, homeopathy, chiropractic, and so forth. They test and review products. They are 100 percent subscriber supported, not taking any paid advertising. A subscription form is available at their website. As a subscriber you can access the current issue online before you receive it in the mail. There is a fourteen-day free trial period online which can be cancelled at any time during that period; instructions for doing so are on the website. If you're dissatisfied with your subscription at any time, you can write to them and they will end your subscription and send you a refund for the balance of your subscription.

For information: whole-dog-journal.com; telephone (toll-free for customer service): 800-424-7887 or (toll-free for subscriptions): 800-829-9165; e-mail (editorial offices): wholedogj@aol.com or (customer service): wholedogj@palmcoastd.com; *Whole Dog Journal*, 1175 Regent St., Alameda, CA 94501 or (for customer service) Belvoir Publications, Inc., 75 Holly Hill Ln., P.O. Box 2626, Greenwich, CT 06836-2626 or for subscription assistance: Subscription Department, P.O. Box 420234, Palm Coast, FL 32142-0234 or (subscription department in Canada) Box 7820 STN Main, London, ON N5Y 5W1, Canada.

YOUR DOG

This monthly newsletter from Tufts University School of Veterinary Medicine is published off-site. The writers consult specialists at Tufts to provide articles of interest, covering topics such as health and behavior. Sample articles are available online. *Your Dog* is sent to subscribers. Call the toll-free number that follows for subscriptions.

For information: tufts.edu/vet/publications/yourdog; telephone (toll-free): 800-829-5116; fax: 203-661-4802; *Your Dog*, Belvoir Publications, 75 Holly Hill Ln., Greenwich, CT 06836.

INTERNATIONAL

CANINE REVIEW

Canine Review was established in 1978 and is Canada's oldest independent dog magazine. Available by subscription, articles cover all aspects of the canine world, including news about the competitive purebred dog. Columnists report on news from across Canada. You can subscribe online or via regular mail. U.S. residents may subscribe as well. The magazine publishes ten issues each year.

For information: canine-review.com; e-mail: editor@canine-review .com; telephone (toll-free): 866-236-0557 or (local): 403-236-0557; fax: 403-236-3271; *Canine Review*, 7003-30 St. SE, Bay 24B, Calgary, AB T2C 1N6, Canada.

CANINE SHOWTIME INTERNATIONAL

Canine Showtime International is a fairly new magazine devoted to training with an emphasis on heelwork to music. The articles are written by contributors from many countries. There are helpful features like the "Trained Dog and Arthritis," a veterinarian's column, "Freestyle Juniors" about kids training their dogs, and much more. The color photos make it even livelier.

For information: e-mail: canineshowtime@aol.com; telephone: 01348 875011; fax: 01348 875013; *Canine Showtime International*, Print House, Parc-y-Shwt, High Street, Fishguard, Pembrokeshire, SA65 9AP, United Kingdom.

DOGS IN CANADA

This award-winning magazine is an arm of the Canadian Kennel Club (CKC) yet they have maintained editorial autonomy. *Dogs in Canada* is published twelve times a year, while its award-winning *Dogs in Canada Annual* is published each November. The annual not only contains articles but is geared to those who want to purchase a dog as well as those who breed them. It also appeals to the thousands of Canadians who love dogs and want to know more about them. Membership in the Canadian Kennel Club includes a subscription to *Dogs in Canada*, but anyone can subscribe to the magazine without joining the CKC. The *Dogs in Canada Annual* is also available at select newsstands.

For information: dogs-in-canada.com; e-mail: info@dogsincanada.com or (for info about joining CKC): info@ckc.ca; telephone: 416-798-9778; fax: 416-798-9671; *Dogs in Canada*, 89 Skyway Ave., Suite 200, Etobicoke, ON M9W 6R4, Canada.

DOGS MONTHLY

Dogs Monthly, launched in 1983, is a British dog magazine that contains articles on a broad range of topics of interest to dog owners. A specific breed is featured each month. Regular features include "Dog Sense," "Dogs Body," a news brief, and more. By giving readers more content, *Dogs Monthly* fills the niche between the weekly dog newspapers—for those in the fancy—and dog magazines that contain personality profiles of famous dog owners and helpful hints. Their articles are informative, tackling topics about dogs as pets, workers, and competitors and exploring the history of their role in the world. *Dogs Monthly* also reports on product news, dog care and training, and the human-dog bond. The magazine appeals to those who are involved in canine sports as well as conformation showing and to those who have mixed breeds as well as those who have purebreds. The philosophy is, "dogs are good for people." You can visit their website and sample the essence of *Dogs Monthly*.

For information: corsini.co.uk/dogsmonthly/index.htm; e-mail: admin @rtc-associates.freeserve.co.uk; telephone: +44 (0) 1344 628269; fax: +44 (0) 1344 622771; *Dogs Monthly*, Ascot House, High Street, Ascot, Berkshire Sl5 7JG, United Kingdom.

DOG WORLD

Dog World is reputedly Britain's top-selling dog newspaper. It includes news, feature articles, reports of dog shows, breed columns, and advertising. It is mainly geared to those who breed and those who show dogs and goes on sale every Friday. The *Dog World Annual* is a glossy, color magazine containing articles and reviews of the world's most successful show dogs. *Dog World*'s comprehensive website has news stories on health issues as well as any and all news pertaining to dogs and dog owners, including the "Pet Travel Scheme" for those who travel abroad. There's a free e-mail newsletter to notify readers of website updates. *Dog World* has dog books, an exhibitor's diary, and more. You can subscribe online using the e-mail address or phone or fax number that follows.

For information: dogworld.co.uk; e-mail: dogworldsubs@cisubs.co.uk; telephone: 0870 444 8626 (Phone hours are Monday through Friday, 8 A.M. to 8 P.M., and Saturday, 9 A.M. to 1 P.M.); fax: 01458 271146.

DOGS TODAY

Dogs Today presents a wide range of features of interest to dog owners, including history involving dogs; articles about service dogs, guide dogs, behavior, training; and even a short story can be found on the pages of this glossy magazine. *Dogs Today* also campaigns for dog welfare.

For information: telephone: 01276 858880; fax: 01276 858860; *Dogs Today*, Pet Subjects Ltd., Town Mill, Bagshot Road, Chobham, Surrey, GU24 8BZ, United Kingdom.

DOGZ ONLINE

The e-zine *Dogz Online* is based in Australia. It features forums for dog discussion and an area where you can profile your show dogs. The focus of the e-zine has mainly been on the show dog, and show results are a regular feature, but the site now has a range of articles pertaining to purebred dogs. The breeds on this website are only those recognized by the Australian National Kennel Council (ANKC) of Australia. The forums are popular and were the catalyst for the formation of the Endangered Dog Breeds Association. You'll also find a section on rescue dogs and a game zone, a marketplace, and more. More features are regularly being added to the site.

For information: dogzonline.com.au, dogzforums.com, and dogs.net .au are all owned by Troy Cumner; e-mail: troy@dogzonline.com.au; P.O. Box 777, Beenleigh Old 4207, Australia.

KENNEL GAZETTE

The *Kennel Gazette* is the monthly magazine of the Kennel Club (in the United Kingdom). The magazine covers everything that the Kennel Club is involved in, including conformation, news from field trials, and other activities, as well as health, news of interest to dog owners, and more.

For information: the-kennel-club.org.uk; The Kennel Club, 1-5 Clarges St., London W1J 8AB, United Kingdom.

OUR DOGS

Our Dogs is a weekly newspaper devoted to show dogs and the people who love them. You can subscribe to the newspaper or to the online version. One of their strong points is the detailed reports of dog shows. They also feature great candid photos of dog fanciers, taken at dog shows.

Their online version is chock full of interesting articles and resources, and part of it is available to nonsubscribers, as is a free e-mail newsletter. *Our Dogs* has show reports, articles, and more. The online version also allows you to shop for the items they sell including diaries, calendars, planners, and books. You can find a lot of information if you are a breeder, exhibitor, or dog lover. Subscribe online or via regular mail.

For information: ourdogs.co.uk; e-mail: subs@ourdogs.co.uk; telephone: (0044) 0870 731 6503; fax: (0044) 0870 731 6504; Our Dogs Publishing, 5 Oxford Road Station Approach, Manchester M60 1SX, United Kingdom.

OZ DOG NEWSPAPER

Oz Dog, Australia's independent canine newspaper, is not related to *Dogz Online* although their websites have the same host. *Oz Dog* features breed profiles, breed pointscores, and articles of interest to people involved in the dog fancy, including late, breaking news. There are also breed profiles. *Oz Dog* is available via subscription or from newsagents and selected places that stock it.

For information: dogzonline.com.au/ozdog/default.htm; e-mail: ozdog@cyber.net.au; telephone (toll-free): 1800 001 073 or (local): 02 9606 8577; fax: 02 9606 8980; *Oz Dog* Newspaper, P.O. Box 58, Austral NSW 2171, Australia.

5

Travel

A t one time, you couldn't travel with your dog; you'd have to look for a boarding kennel. And while some people might still opt to do that, many more prefer the company of their canine companion. Happily, some places recognize that a growing segment of the traveling population prefers to have their dogs with them, so they will make the experience a pleasurable one for both dog and owner. As long as owners are careful to leave the hotel room clean and not allow their dog to cause any damage during their stay, everyone will continue to benefit from a pet-friendly policy.

Remember to obtain a health certificate from your veterinarian within ten days of leaving on your trip, as well as proof of up-to-date vaccinations. A copy of your dog's health records will be valuable if your dog becomes sick on the road. You'll also want to travel with your dog's food and bottled water to avoid intestinal upsets. Keep a first-aid kit with you in case of an emergency, and ask your veterinarian if she or he knows of a veterinarian in the area to which you'll be traveling in case of an emergency.

Carry a current photograph of your dog with you in case he gets lost. Don't forget to take along the number of one of the poison-control hotlines. You can tape it to your first-aid kit or keep it in your wallet. The ASPCA's Animal Poison Center can be reached at 888-426-4435. Specially trained veterinary toxicologists—who have an extensive collection of scientific journals and books available along with sophisticated databases—are on duty around the clock. The hotline is available twenty-four hours a day, seven days a week. They do charge a $45 consultation fee that you can put on your credit card.

For your dog's safety, he should be wearing an identification tag and should be either microchipped or have a tattoo. Don't forget to register the microchip or tattoo with the appropriate company so that you can be tracked down, should your dog get lost and be found by someone who calls one of the registries.

If you're driving, be sure to stop and walk your dog on a leash every few hours. You should also have a flashlight for nighttime walks. Carry paper towels with you along with a cleaner that breaks down enzymes, in case your dog has an accident or vomits while in a hotel or motel. If you use wee-wee pads or newspapers for elimination, set them up on the tile floor in the bathroom. Being a thoughtful traveler will make it easier for every owner who travels with his or her dog.

If your dog likes his crate—and it should be a safe haven that he enjoys—bring it along. Not only is it a safer way to travel in the car, but he'll appreciate having his own place in the hotel or motel room where he feels safe. Alternately, your dog might be happy with a doggie seat belt. If your dog is small, some very nice, sturdy, doggie car seats are available. Sometimes this is helpful for a dog who gets carsick. Some dogs need to be able to see out, the way a seasick person feels better when looking at the horizon.

Take your dog for a walk or run as soon as you check in so he'll have a chance to eliminate as well as stretch his legs. And when you leave the room, leave the TV or radio on if you can't take him with you along with one of your shirts or nightgowns so your scent will remain with him. Be certain that he has no escape routes and that he has toys to keep him occupied while you're away from the room. Keep him on a leash at all times when in public areas.

HOW TO PUT TOGETHER A FIRST-AID KIT

Start with a box that has compartments so you can find things easily when you need them in a hurry. A fishing tackle box is a good choice and reasonably priced. Make a trip to your local drugstore and gather an assortment of items you'll need just in case. Remember to have gauze pads and gauze tape, cotton balls, and roll cotton. Add a bottle of hydrogen peroxide, but be sure to check the date on it and change the bottle once it becomes outdated. Add hydrocortisone ointment, an antibiotic ointment, scissors, tweezers, magnifying glass, a flashlight or a penlight, eyewash, silver nitrate, a thermometer (oral and rectal ones can both be used rectally), oral syringes, balanced electrolyte fluid, and baby food (meat works best). Add the last two items just before your trip. Don't forget to have a large towel, exam gloves, one-inch-wide tape (you'll need this in addition to the gauze tape), rolls of elastic wrap, an emergency ice pack, and aspirin. Be certain you know the correct dose for your dog and be sure he can tolerate it before you leave on your trip.

Doggie first-aid kits are available commercially. The Kennel Club in England has one that's compact and contains basic items. You can contact The Kennel Club, 1-5 Clarges St., London W1J 8AB, United Kingdom. You can phone them at 0870 6066750. Medi-Pet First Aid Kits are available at major pet supply chain stores in the United States, as well as through online retailers, and come in both basic and deluxe versions. The standard kit contains scissors, nonadherent dressing, medium dressing, tweezers, saline minipads, and more. The deluxe version contains everything the standard kit has plus an instant cold pack, emergency blanket, magnifying glass, iodine prep solution, and more.

IF YOU NEED A VETERINARIAN

To locate a veterinarian at your destination or along the way, ask your own veterinarian for referrals or ask friends. You can also visit the American Animal Hospital Association's informative website for pet owners, healthypet.com, where you can use the veterinarian locator to find hospitals that have gone to the extra effort of being approved by AAHA, thereby becoming a member hospital. AAHA has more than twenty-nine thousand veterinary care providers and more than three thousand hospitals actively participate in AAHA's voluntary evaluation program. Individual veterinarians are also AAHA members.

DOG TAGS

Dog tags can be purchased from a variety of places, including local pet supply stores. Many veterinarians also have order forms for regular tags.

DOG-E-TAG™

Dog-e-Tag, "the world's first digital dog tag" currently for dogs fifteen pounds and over, is a digital tag that's 1⅜ inches (36 millimeters) around and weighs a mere ¾ ounce (21 grams). It's worn like a metal tag, but there's nothing common about a tag that can hold up to forty lines of information, such as multiple phone numbers, e-mail address, the dog's county license number if it's allowed by your county, city or state, as well as rabies vaccination number, veterinarian contact, neighbors, medical and dietary information, and more. It has a high-resolution display that you can see when either of two buttons is pushed and it comes in a variety of fashionable colors.

When you're traveling, you can update the tag to include local contact information. You can also use a personal identification number (PIN) to prevent stored information from being changed by anyone else. And, it can be programmed in your choice of languages: English, French, German, Italian, or Spanish. The tags have a shock-resistant case and are waterproof to 165 feet (50 meters) and they function in a wide range of temperatures. The lens is scratch-resistant and the display automatically illuminates for nighttime or low-light reading conditions. You can replace the battery yourself.

Dog-e-Tag has a one-year warranty to the original owner against defects in material, workmanship, and assembly. You can find more information at their website. You can order on the Web, via regular mail (there's a downloadable order form), or via telephone or fax.

For information: dog-e-tag.com; e-mail: e-tag@etagsllc.com; telephone (toll-free): 866-DOG-ETAG; fax: 805-477-1655; Dog-e-Tag, 5 N. Pacific Ave., Ventura, CA 93001.

E-Z-U'S SIGNS, INC.

This company, based in Dover, Delaware, makes tags in various styles. You can purchase tags that hang from the dog's collar or the plate type, that's attached to the collar itself. Collar tags are engraved on one side only. Other tags have engraving on both sides available; however information is engraved on one side unless another layout is requested. ID's come with an s-hook or split-ring to attach the tag to the collar. Collar tags come with rivets to attach to the collar. Note that you'll need a hammer to install the rivets. This company also makes plastic crate signs in a variety of colors, as well as license plate frames, with lettering in a choice of black or chrome frame.

For information: ezusigns.com; e-mail: signman@ezusigns.com; telephone (toll-free): 800-823-9519; fax: 302-677-0838; E-Z-U's Signs, Inc., 5470 Bayside Dr., Dover, DE 19901.

TATTOO REGISTRIES

Keeping a tag on your dog is always a good idea, but you might want to consider a more permanent means of identifying your dog in case he is ever lost. A tattoo, which is usually placed on the lower abdomen, is a permanent means of identification. You register the tattoo number with one of the registries and anyone who finds your dog can phone in with the number and you will be contacted.

NATIONAL DOG REGISTRY

Established in 1966, this is the oldest tattoo registry in the United States. They will register pets in the United States, Canada, and Puerto Rico. They can be reached at their toll-free number. If your pet is lost or stolen, they will be there to help you twenty-four hours a day, seven days a week, every day of the year. The slogan on their emblem is "ethics, dependability, and honor." Lifetime membership is only $38 and it will protect every tattooed pet you will ever own. They charge a nominal fee for changing records. The membership fee will also give you access to NDR's other services, which include a pet-owner's kit, unlimited access to their missing pet counseling service, support products, and more. NDR accepts numbers from other registries, so you don't need to change the tattoo number if you want to register your dog with NDR.

For information: natldogregistry.com; e-mail: info@natldogregistry .com; telephone (toll-free): 800-NDR-DOGS; fax: 845-679-2355; NDR, P.O. Box 116, Woodstock, NY 12498-0116.

TATTOO-A-PET™

Tattoo-a-Pet claims to be the world's largest tattoo network for pet protection. Established in 1972, they have a $35, lifetime fee with a charge of $10 for additional pets. They also have a hotline number tag service available with no tattoo for $25 for all animals with a charge of $2 for each additional tag.

For information: tattoo-a-pet.com; e-mail: info@tattoo-a-pet.com; telephone (toll-free): 800-TATTOOS or (local): 954-581-5834; fax: 954-581-0056; Tattoo-a-Pet, 6571 S.W. 20th Ct., Ft. Lauderdale, FL 33317.

MICROCHIPPING

A microchip is a tiny computer chip about the size of a grain of rice and has a permanent identification number on it. It is tiny enough to fit in a hypodermic needle and is injected under the animal's skin where it stays permanently. No two animals ever have the same number which is registered with the company. A special scanner with a radio signal allows someone to read the number.

AVID

AVID is an acronym that stands for American Veterinary Identification Devices, founded by the veterinarian who developed Animal Intensive Care Unit. The microchip number is registered with AVID, along with your contact information, your veterinarian's name, and the name of someone else they can contact if your animal is found and they can't reach you. You register the number with PETtrac, a global computer-ized tracking system for companion animals identified with the AVID microchip. It costs $15 to register one pet and $40 to register up to eight pets. There is a $6 charge for information changes. The cost of the microchip is extra and your veterinarian sets that fee. Their web-site contains answers to frequently asked questions, as well as a section to find a veterinarian who can microchip your pet with an AVID microchip, and areas for people who have found a lost pet or are look-ing for a lost pet.

For information: avidid.com; e-mail: avid@avidid.com; telephone (toll-free): 800-336-2843 or (local): 909-371-7505; Avid Identifica-tion Systems, Inc., 3179 Hamner Ave., Norco, CA 92860-1983.

HOME AGAIN

Home Again microchips are registered with the AKC's Companion Animal Recovery program (CAR), which maintains a national database available twenty-four hours daily, every day of the year. The lost pet can be scanned at an animal shelter or a participating veterinarian's clinic. The ID number is then called into AKC-CAR at their toll-free number and the pet owner is notified at once. The owner is asked to provide an alternate person to notify if the owner can't be reached. AKC-CAR also maintains an e-mail address where found pets can be reported. Any pet (including cats) can be enrolled, not just purebred dogs. Home Again can be purchased online, as can enrollment in the CAR database for $63.50. The microchip can also be purchased directly from veterinary clinics, but the price may vary. If you purchase it through your veterinarian, the enrollment in the CAR database is an additional $12.50. Assistance dogs can be enrolled free of charge. Some shelters offer discounts for micro-chipping to people who adopt shelter pets. Home Again's website pro-vides information, general articles of interest about pets, and names of veterinarians who can microchip your pet.

For information: homeagainid.com; e-mail: support@homeagainid .com or (to report found pets): found@akc.org; telephone (toll-free for Home Again): 800-887-7310 or (toll-free for AKC Companion Animal Recovery Program): 800-252-7894.

INTERNATIONAL

PETLOG

In 1995, the Kennel Club in the United Kingdom launched Petlog, a service dedicated to owners of microchipped animals. It is somewhat akin to the AKC-CAR program. Petlog provides a lifetime recovery service and is the largest plan of any kind in the U.K. The microchip is implanted by veterinarians or other authorized individuals. Petlog's database—where the owner's information is recorded, including an alternate contact person—is administered by the Kennel Club. Petlog has an estimated 86 percent success rate in reuniting lost pets with their owners. The Kennel Club now offers existing and future customers the opportunity to pay a onetime, all-inclusive fee of £10 for Petlog Plus, which includes all future changes to address details (instead of the regular £5 charge) and updates on vaccination information. They expect to add more services such as an e-subscription service containing reminders and newsletters. Additionally, Petlog Plus customers will receive a membership wallet, containing documentation relating to the pet, including a useful telephone-number sheet and what to do if a pet is lost. Petlog operates twenty-four hours a day, seven days a week. Several microchip manufacturers work with Petlog. Information can be found using a link at the Kennel Club's website. Once you reach that portion of the website, you'll see a link for European Pet Network.

For information: the-kennel-club.org.uk or europetnet.com; Petlog, 4A Alton House, Alton House Office Park, Gatehouse Way, Aylesbury, Bucks, HP19 8XU, United Kingdom.

TRAVELING BY PLANE WITH YOUR DOG

If you're traveling by plane, keep in mind a few things. If your dog is small (approximately less than twenty-one pounds) he can travel onboard with you, but the carrier must stay under the seat. When you arrive at the airport, you'll have to clear security with your pet. He'll have to be taken out of his carrier and held as you walk through the metal detector while the carrier is put through the x-ray machine. He can go back into the carrier once it has cleared the x-ray machine and you have cleared the metal detector.

Be sure to exercise your dog before entering the airport so he has an opportunity to relieve himself. You can also take newspaper or a wee-wee pad into the restroom, let him relieve himself on that, and then properly dispose of it. Do not, however, put a wee-wee pad in the bottom of his carrier, because it is scented to give him the idea of where to go and will make him feel that he has to relieve himself while he's in the carrier.

If your dog is too large to carry aboard, you'll have to check him in as baggage. Be certain to have him in an airline-approved crate with a name tag properly secured to the crate containing your identification information. You can't feed him before the flight (he'll need to fly on an empty stomach), but secure a small bag of his food to the crate just in case his flight is delayed or he's stuck somewhere in transit. Add a note for the airline crew so they'll know that the food is for that purpose. You can also attach a little bag with some of his cookies to the crate, along with a note to the airline personnel.

Attach a water dish to the crate, and put ice cubes in it at the last minute; the ice will melt giving your dog fresh, cold water during the flight. If you can teach him to use one of the water bottles used by rabbits (the animal licks it and it slowly releases the water into the animal's mouth) it can be secured to the crate and the water won't spill. You can use a larger bag and put a bottle of water in there so the airline personnel can give him bottled water if his flights are delayed or rerouted. Bottled water will be safer for him than tap water because he won't be used to the water in another place.

The newer aircraft baggage compartments can have the atmosphere adjusted just like the passenger compartment, but there are a couple of important things that you should know. Ask if they're carrying dried ice for any reason. Be certain that your dog is *not* with dried ice and have them put his crate into another compartment if necessary. When you board the aircraft, ask the flight attendant to notify the pilot that you have a dog aboard and ask him or her to monitor the atmosphere in the baggage compartment. Alternatively, you can hand the attendant a typewritten letter to give to the pilot, making this request. Your dog should not be tranquilized before a flight. And be sure that your dog is very familiar with his carrier or travel crate well before the trip. You can do this by putting a comfy pad, blanket, or towel in there for him to curl up on along with a favorite toy or two.

AIRLINE OPTIONS

Now that you've taken care of all safety precautions, where can you go? Well, the sky's the limit.

COMPANION AIR®

Speaking of the sky being the limit, there is now an airline dedicated to transporting pets. They've started with shuttle flights and expect to expand into longer flights. And they have charter options. They fly prop planes and each one has a separate, specially designed area for the pets with attendants who look after their needs and safety. Pets don't travel in the cargo hold on Companion Air. There's room for two passengers in the pet area. Once airborne, the travelers in the passenger cabin can walk back to the pet cabin to visit with their pets. Human airfares are 20 percent less than pet airfares to encourage owners to come along on the flight. Special treats and toys are aboard for both pets and owners.

For information: companionair.com; telephone: 561-470-0970; fax: 561-483-0970; Companion Air Corporation, 22344 Siesta Key Dr., Boca Raton, FL 33428.

INTERNATIONAL

PETS BY AIR

This family-run business transports pets around New Zealand and around the world. At Pets by Air, "We aim to anticipate an owners every 'wish and worry' as well as smooth the way for their pet to have an enjoyable and worry-free trip from one place to another." At an owner's request, they will often use homeopathic remedies to help the pet cope with the stress of moving. Crates used in the aircraft are custom built and meet International Air Transport Association standards. The dogs fly on regular passenger planes and can accompany their owners on the same flight or travel alone. They travel in the bulk hold, which is specially temperature controlled for animals. This airline also keeps the hold at a low light to help keep the dogs comfortable, which encourages them to sleep during the flight.

For information: petsbyair.com; e-mail: annette@petsbyair.com; telephone (international): 64 9 520 6297, (New Zealand): 09-5206297, or (mobile): 025-520629; fax: New Zealand 09-5204923; Annette and Troy Ironside, Pets by Air, P.O. Box 17048, Greenlane 1003, Auckland, New Zealand.

TAKING A TOUR WITH YOUR DOG

Traveling with your dog can be a lot of fun, and even more so when you travel with a group of like-minded people and their dogs. Whether it's an adventure trip or a group of travelers with their canines going off to a dog show, group travel can relieve some of the pressures of taking a trip. The vacation is planned for you and includes hotels, transportation, some meals, and a tour leader. A tour allows you to meet others who share your interests and pleasure in traveling with a dog.

BLUE SKY DOGS

This fairly new company, founded in 2003, offers travel for dogs and their owners, as well as boarding for dogs, in the New York area. They claim to be New York's first and only canine adventure and dog travel company. They kicked off this venture with the first of their Best Friend Weekends with a trip to the Catskill Mountains in March 2004. Vacations are all-inclusive and adventures include a guided hike with your dog. Trips are limited to approximately twenty-five people and fifteen dogs. The company was begun by Tammy McCarley and her dog, Sienna. Day trips and overnight boarding, which McCarley calls "Slumber Parties," are also planned. The Adventure Days are for dogs only and are play days for dogs in a wilderness setting. These trips include round-trip transportation, digital photos, fresh natural treats, and cold filtered water. Blue Sky Dogs is planning to begin holding Pet First Aid Courses as well as Owner Adventure Day Trips.

For information: blueskydogsny.com; e-mail: info@blueskydogsny .com; telephone: 212-532-DOGS.

FRESH POND TRAVEL

This full-service travel agency places a heavy emphasis on dog-related travel, booking both individual and group tours to most of the important dog shows in the world, including Crufts in England; Westminster in New York; the World Show, which is in a different European capital each year; and the Irish Kennel Club show in Dublin on St. Patrick's Day. They also produce seminars on cruise ships and at resorts. You can travel to these events with or without dogs, depending upon your preference and the individual event. Prices for trips range from approximately $150 for land-based seminars to approximately $2,500 for something as special as the Scottish Kennel Club Show in conjunction with the Edinburgh Festival each August. Most trips cost approximately $1,500. Clients receive mailings several times each year with the latest offerings. The information on upcoming trips and seminars can also be found on their website. If you wish to receive information from time to time, you can e-mail your name and address to either of the addresses that follow and be placed on a mailing list.

For information: dogshowtravel.com; e-mail: freshpondtravel@ verizon.net or info@dogshowtravel.com; telephone (toll-free): 877-SHOWDOG; Dog Show Travel, 344 Boston Post Rd., Marlboro, MA 01752.

ROVIN' WITH ROVER

If you're connected to the Internet, point your browser to the Rovin' with Rover website to get in on the fun of taking a tour with your dog. Based in Ohio, all tours currently depart from Ohio cities; however, the company plans to branch out. They usually do one- or two-day tours through Ohio, New York, Pennsylvania, and West Virginia, traveling by deluxe motor coach to the destinations and then by train, tram, hay wagon, or boat. They also do walking and driving tours and receive special permission to go into museums and shops such as the Zippo Museum in Bradford, Pennsylvania; the I Love Lucy museum in Jamestown, New York; the Palace Theatre and a Harley Davidson shop in Gowanda, New York; a carousel gift shop and factory in Mansfield, Ohio; and an empty penitentiary and toy museum in Wheeling, West Virginia. They have navigated a cornfield maze, browsed pottery shops, toured and sampled various wineries, and held Halloween parties with canine costume contests. They've dined in a renovated train station turned restaurant, in the Overlook Museum in West Virginia, aboard luxurious boats, as well as in outdoor pavilions and parks. In addition to the website, you can get on a mailing list or obtain a brochure. The tours cost approximately $100 per day, which includes the bus, admission fees, a meal(s), and guide service. If you don't have Internet service, you can write to them to request information.

For information: rovinwithrover.com; Rovin' with Rover, 9461 Briar St., Streetsboro, OH 44241.

SUN DOG EXPRESS DOG SLED TOURS

If you've wanted to try dog sledding, you'll have an opportunity in Fairbanks, Alaska. The activities aren't restricted to the winter months. They offer summer demonstrations and rides along with a presentation that includes history, equipment, and stories about mushing. They offer a variety of winter tours, differing in length. You can even attend a half-day mushing school if you would really like to immerse yourself in the experience.

For information: mosquitonet.com/~sleddog; telephone: 907-479-6983; Sun Dog Express, P.O. Box 10663, Fairbanks, AK 99710-0663.

INTERNATIONAL

COACHES TO SHOWS

If you're in the United Kingdom and have a yen to travel to dog shows, Coaches to Shows will take you on that special trip. Their coach tours to various European locations feature executive coaches that are specially fitted with dog crates. The bus tour includes one cage free, but there is a charge for extra cages if you're bringing more than one dog. You'll need to bring your own to use in the hotels. They also fly groups to shows such as the Westminster Kennel Club Dog Show in New York. They also travel to the World Show and the Euro Dog Show. If a country isn't covered by the Pet Passport Scheme—which allows a dog to travel in certain European countries by providing proof of good health without having to enter quarantine—owners can travel without dogs and enjoy the show itself without showing their own dogs.

For information: coaches-to-shows.co.uk; e-mail: john.r.wright@ btinternet.com; telephone: +44 8970 046 6655.

DOG SHOWS

Whether you show your own dog or just enjoy seeing dogs, going to a show is always fun. If your dog isn't entered, you won't be able to bring him to the show grounds. However, you will certainly have fun watching the judging and visiting the vendors' booths to shop for all manner of things for you and your dog. Shows are held virtually everywhere but some shows are big, special, and attract people from all over the world.

CRUFTS

According to the *Guinness Book of World Records*, Crufts is the world's biggest dog show. It attained that distinction in 2003 when more than 20,000 dogs and 128,998 people attended over the four-day period. Five hundred forty-three dogs from twenty countries around the world were there to compete. Taking place in March each year at Birmingham's huge National Exhibition Center, it fills five show halls and runs over four days and evenings. Along with conformation competition, you'll see demonstrations and competitions of virtually every dog sport plus police, search-and-rescue, as well as assistance dog demonstrations. The wildly popular Discover Dogs display has an incredible array of breeds on display with information about the breed, its country of origin, and breed club members present to answer questions. Literally hundreds of vendors fill each show hall. Plan to bring an extra suitcase because it's virtually impossible to resist the international shopping with vendors from several countries bringing wonderful things for you and your dog. Group and best-in-show tickets are at a premium, so reserve early. Tickets go on sale as early as September. More information is available at The Kennel Club's wonderfully user-friendly website, which has an e-mail form on the site.

For information: the-kennel-club.org.uk; telephone: 0870 606 6750; fax: 020 7518 1058; The Kennel Club, 1 Clarges St., London W1J 8AB, United Kingdom.

WESTMINSTER KENNEL CLUB DOG SHOW

The United States' first champions-only dog show, Westminster Kennel Club Dog Show changed its rules so that only champions can compete. It is also the second oldest continuous sporting event in the United States; only the Kentucky Derby is older. It takes place in New York City's Madison Square Garden for two days and evenings each February. The dogs are in the benching area all day, which means that you can walk through and see them being groomed or resting. You'll also find the vendors set up in this area behind the show rings. Tickets for group judging at night are difficult to come by, so make plans early if you want to stay for groups and best-in-show judging. Otherwise, you will have to plan to watch the show at your hotel on cable television.

For information: westminsterkennelclub.org; e-mail: write@wkcpr .org; Westminster Kennel Club, Public Relations Department, 149 Madison Ave., Suite 803, New York, NY 10016.

WORLD DOG SHOW

The Federation Cynologique Internationale (FCI) is the name of the World Canine Organization. FCI includes seventy-nine members and contract partners (one member from each country) that issue their own pedigrees and train their own judges. The FCI makes sure the pedigrees and judges are mutually recognized by all FCI members. International Championships can be attained at their shows. It should be noted that the AKC is not a member of FCI.

A World Dog Show takes place in a different host country each year. Dogs that win can be called World Winners. The show is not held during any one specific month. Information is posted well in advance at the FCI website.

For information: fci.be; e-mail: info@fci.be; telephone: +32.71.59 .12.38; fax: +32.71.59.22.29; FCI, Place Albert 1er, 13, B-6530 Thuin, Belgium.

FUN TRIPS WITH YOUR DOG

Some trips with your dog can be more adventuresome than others. For those who are athletic and enjoy a more active lifestyle, here are trips that you and your dog can share.

DOG PADDLING ADVENTURES

Have you ever thought about going canoeing with your dog? Dog Paddling Adventures is Canada's first outdoor adventure company specifically catering to dogs and their owners. They have paddling, as well as winter adventures like skijoring and kicksledding, and they offer spring and fall hiking trips. All of the adventures are designed for people who share an interest and enthusiasm for the wilderness and dogs.

For information: dogpaddlingadventures.com; e-mail: jessie@dog paddlingadventures.com; telephone: 905-477-2493; Dog Paddling Adventures, 177 Idema Rd., Markham, ON, L3R 1A9, Canada.

SOUTHWIND KAYAK CENTER

If you enjoy kayaking, you might consider taking your canine friend with you. As with canoeing, he'll need a life jacket for safety just as you do. Southwind Kayak Center can get you started. While some dogs like to ride on the bow of the kayak, others prefer to ride in the lower, more stable cockpit. Each dog will react differently to the adventure, whether with high spirits or preferring to sleep and enjoy the serenity of the water.

Information, including tips to help you and your dog friend get started and how to introduce him to his life jacket and the kayak can be found at their website, along with activities that you can do together while on your kayak adventure. Southwind also provides suggestions as to which types of kayaks and canoes are best for people who want to take their dog along. They will also give you information about which skills your dog will need to learn, such as learning to shake off all the water from his coat when you want him to, so you won't get an unnecessary soaking. And, they'll tell you what you'll need to bring along for your dog. If you're in the area, the store has kayak classes, rentals, and more. *For information:* southwindkayaks.com; e-mail: info@southwind kayaks.com/kayakdogs.html; telephone (toll-free): 800-SOUTHWIND or (local): 949-261-0200; Southwind Kayak Center, 17855 Skypark Cr. #A, Irvine, CA 92614.

SUN VALLEY, IDAHO

Interestingly, Sun Valley, Idaho, calls itself the most dog-friendly resort in the United States. The climate certainly allows year-round fun with your canine companion, including some snowshoe and cross-country ski trails on which dogs are welcome in winter. Many of the resorts, hotels, motels, and bed-and-breakfasts will welcome your dog if you give them advance notice that you're traveling with your canine companion.

The Sun Valley Animal Center has doggie days available and your companion won't be bored because they have a playground and plenty of toys to amuse him until you return. Restaurants with outdoor dining areas have special sections where you can bring your dog while you dine, and your dog will be served a bowl of water and some biscuits while you're eating so he needn't feel left out. Many places reportedly have water bowls available if your dog is thirsty and many businesses will give your dog a biscuit. This is a place where dogs are appreciated.

Dogs in the area are active in rescue and specially trained avalanche dogs are working in the Sun Valley area during ski season. *For information:* visitsunvalley.com; e-mail: chamberinfo@visitsun valley.com; telephone (toll-free): 800-634-3347; Sun Valley/Ketchum, Chamber and Visitors Bureau, P.O. Box 2420, Sun Valley, ID 83353.

GO TO CAMP WITH YOUR DOG

If you think that camp is just fun for children, then you're missing out on a lot of fun. Adults and their dogs can share some wonderful experiences at camps designed specifically for dogs and their people. Needless to say, all activities revolve around the dogs.

CAMP GONE TO THE DOGS®

One of the earliest camping programs for dogs and their people, Camp Gone to the Dogs was started in 1990 by Honey Loring. They offer a wide variety of activities, including obedience, agility, canine musical freestyle, herding, hunting, breed handling, and Tellington Touch. They have forty to fifty activities daily, and you have the opportunity to try whatever you'd like with your dog. Happily, the camp uses only positive training methods. Puppies to seniors are welcome. They do not have an e-mail address, but you can visit their website, phone them, or contact them via mail.

For information: http://camp-gone-tothe-dogs.com; telephone: 802-387-5673 (Phone hours are Monday through Friday, 9 A.M. to 5 P.M., EST.); Camp Gone to the Dogs, P.O. Box 600, Putney, VT 05346.

CAMP WINARIBBUN

Camp Winaribbun is located in Nevada on beautiful Lake Tahoe. Hikes, agility, tracking, carting, games, and programs on homeopathy, search and rescue, as well as pet therapy are just some of the things you can do at this camp. There's something for every age group and energy level. *For information:* campw.com; e-mail: info@campw.com; telephone: 775-348-8412; fax: 775-329-0629; Camp Winaribbun, P.O. Box 50300, Reno, NV 89513.

DOG DAYS OF WISCONSIN

If you long for a Midwest vacation with your dog, Dog Days of Wisconsin may be what you're looking for. Activities include "Barks and Crafts," "Vet Talk," dog first aid, obedience, agility, dental hygiene, flyball, and Frisbee among other activities. Puppies to seniors are welcome. For more information, visit their website.

For information: dogcamp.com; e-mail: summercamp@dogcamp.com; telephone (toll-free): 800-CAMP-4-DOGS or (local): 262-521-2005; Dog Days of Wisconsin, LLC, 235 W. Greenfield Ave., Waukesha, WI 53186.

INTERNATIONAL

CAMP DOGWOULD

If you're in Canada, or would like to visit a dog camp in Canada, you can check out Camp Dogwould for a weekend of fun, lectures, and training. You'll have a wide array of activities from which to choose, including rally obedience, regular obedience, power heeling/ring prep, agility, freestyle, flyball, tracking, fun games and tricks class, search and rescue, and Tellington Touch. They also have a CKC Good Neighbour Test, Canadian Good Citizen Test, Herding Instinct Test, and Obedience, Agility & Rally-O Fun matches. Their motto is "your dog would love it." With all of those choices, that makes perfect sense. Since there's a beach area, you'll probably want to bring your swimsuit. *For information:* campdogwould.com; e-mail: info@campdogwould .com; telephone: 613-632-6502; fax: 613-632-7937; Camp Dogwould, 2886 Front Rd. East, Hawkesbury, ON, K6A 2R2, Canada.

HOTELS, MOTELS, RESORTS, AND INNS

This is just a sampling of some of the many places that will welcome your canine traveling companion (most welcome felines, too).

BAY PALM RESORT

With a firm "Pets Are Welcome" in capital letters on their website, there is no doubt that the Bay Palm Resort in St. Petersburg, Florida, is serious about their pet policy. They are located directly on the Intracoastal Waterway overlooking the bay. A twelve-hundred-square-foot fishing and boat dock are available for the use of guests. Recently renovated, a heated, freshwater swimming pool has been added to the property. They have large, one-bedroom suites, efficiencies, or an overnight motel room. All accommodations are air conditioned, and the one-bedroom suites and efficiency units have refrigerators and microwave ovens. Each has a color television, direct-dial telephones, and weekly maid service. The rooms also come equipped with a surge-protected personal computer hookup. Just across from the Bay Palm Resort, you'll find five miles of white-sand beaches along the Gulf of

Mexico. Shops and restaurants are within walking distance and cultural attractions can be enjoyed in the nearby Tampa Bay area. Special rates are available during the fall season.

For information: baypalmresort.com; e-mail: baypalmresort@aol.com; telephone: 727-360-7642; fax: 727-360-6517; Bay Palm Resort, 4237 Gulf Blvd., St. Pete Beach, FL 33706.

CENTER COURT INN

Center Court Historic Inn and Cottages in Key West, Florida, are situated on a quiet lane in Historic Old Town. Their units are mere steps from each other and from the attractions of Duval Street. Owned by a registered nurse who supervised the design, renovation, and decoration of the historic cottages, which date back to the 1880s, the properties received Awards of Excellence from the Key West Historical Preservation Society in 1994. That same year, AAA awarded them the coveted Three Diamonds designation. Center Court Inn has gardens, a heated pool, spa, exercise pavilion, private sun deck, and a fish-lily pond. All rooms and suites have private baths with hair dryers, CATV, phone, fans, air conditioning, in-room safe, and beach bags. The cottages also have full kitchens, gas barbecue grills, and private yards. Pets are welcome, four dogs are in residence. Daphne, a Parson Russell Terrier, loves to play and surf the pool. Holly, a senior Black Lab, likes to sleep. Sasha, an ASCOB Cocker Spaniel, is shy but wears hand-decorated collars. An Italian Greyhound named Julius rounds out the bunch. You can usually find all four dogs lounging around the Center Court's office.

For information: http://centercourtkw.com; e-mail: info@centercourt kw.com; telephone (toll-free): 800-797-8787 or (local): 305-296-9292; Center Court Historic Inn and Cottages, 915 Center St., Key West, FL 33040. (Office hours are seven days a week, 9 A.M. to 7 P.M., EST.)

THE COTTAGES, BOAT BASIN

The Cottages, Boat Basin, are on the captivating island of Nantucket, off the coast of Massachusetts. Set near the waterfront, this delightful grouping of cottages welcomes your four-footed companion in their pet-friendly cottages. In fact, they refer to their dog-friendly cottages as the "woof cottages."

Upon checking in, your dog will receive a basket full of treats and toys, including a complimentary Cottages dog collar. For your companion's comfort, he'll sleep on a Blissful Bed. The cottage will also have food and water bowls in the cottage awaiting his arrival. You will receive pet-oriented information on check-in including a cautionary note about Lyme disease and a list of phone numbers for veterinarians as well as pet sitters and dog walkers.

They have an extensive lawn area and a small portion of beach access behind the cottage, so your dog can enjoy the holiday just as much as you will. They do ask that you clean up after your own dog and to make that easier for you, a trash can and doggie bags are provided.

Like a hotel, there is daily housekeeping between 9 A.M. and 4 P.M. You are asked to call the front desk daily to arrange a convenient time for them to come so they won't startle your pet.

Dogs should be kept on leash at all times when you're on public property in Nantucket, which is an extremely dog-friendly community. Dogs seem to be everywhere. Remember to properly dispose of your dog's waste. Keeping Nantucket clean and pleasant will ensure that dog owners will continue to be able to enjoy the island. Remember that Nantucket has some rare and endangered ground-nesting birds, so be sure your dog is on leash while on the beach and under your watchful eye so he won't disturb the birds. Nantucket's bike trails, which lead you around and across the island in every direction, are suitable for pets, as long as they're kept on leash. Transportation to Nantucket, whether by their commuter airline or by ferry, is also pet friendly. Cats are also welcome and receive their own gift basket with a bandanna in it instead of a collar. A litter box, scoop, and litter can be arranged.

For information: thecottagesnantucket.com; telephone (toll-free): 866-838-9253 or (local): 508-325-1499; fax: 508-325-1378; The Cottages, Boat Basin, One Old South Wharf; P.O. Box 1139, Nantucket, MA 02554.

CYPRESS INN

The Cypress Inn, located in exquisite Carmel-by-the-Sea, California, has been co-owned for more than twenty years by actress/singer Doris Day, her son Terry Melcher, and their business partner in the venture, Dennis LeVett. Day has said that she bought the hotel to change their policy to a pet-friendly one.

The Mediterranean façade, garden court, and lobby are charming, made more so for dogs by the bowl of dog biscuits kept at the front desk. They are located near Carmel's equally pet-friendly beach, one of the few in California where dogs are allowed to run off leash. And they maintain a list of nearby restaurants where pets are welcome in the outdoor dining area; some of them will provide your dog with a water bowl and biscuits while you dine and some have a special doggie menu. The rooms have been remodeled and the hotel has been newly expanded. Cats are every bit as welcome, although dogs are in the majority visiting the hotel. Many people choose to stay here traveling to the area for nearby dog shows. The charge for pets is merely $20, per day, and $15 for each additional pet. Personal service extends to the doggie traveler with nightly biscuit turn-down service and a pet blanket which can either be placed on the bed to save the bedspread or your dog can curl up on it on the floor. Pet sitters are available and the inn maintains a list of independent contractors.

For the human companion, Cypress Inn features the charm of afternoon cream tea, complete with homemade scones, a daily ritual from 2 P.M. to 3:45 P.M. in the lobby, library area, and courtyard. Reservations are required. It is very reasonably priced at $15 per person. Rules of the house for dogs state that pets must not be left alone in the room at any time or under any circumstances; they must be on lead or in the owner's keeping at all times while in public areas of the Cypress Inn; and they are not allowed on the furniture in the guest rooms or public areas. If you forget anything for your pet, the inn can probably supply it. At Christmas, each pet receives a gift.

For information: cypress-inn.com; e-mail: info@cypress-inn.com; telephone (toll-free for reservations in the United States and Canada): 800-443-7443 or (local): 831-624-3871; fax: 831-624-8216; The Cypress Inn, Lincoln and 7th, P.O. Box Y, Carmel-by-the-Sea, CA 93921.

DOG-FRIENDLY LODGING ON WHIDBEY ISLAND, WASHINGTON

This site lists several pet-friendly places, including a bed-and-breakfast inn, a guesthouse, cottages, and an off-leash park. Despite the rustic setting, the accommodations are quite complete with amenities such as a gourmet kitchen, TVs and VCRs, and a stereo/CD player in one beachfront property. Pets must, of course, be well behaved. Individual contact information for the properties can be found at the website. They also seek volunteers to help keep the area pristine. There's also a listing of park locations on Whidbey Island as well as a link for News from FETCH, which is a Washington State nonprofit organization dedicated to providing this area with places where people can exercise their dogs off-leash without disturbing others.

For information: whidbey.net/fetch/lodging.htm; e-mail: fetch@whidbey.com; telephone (for FETCH): 360-321-4049; fax: 360-321-2401; FETCH, P.O. Box 212, Langley, WA 98260.

INN BY THE SEA

The Inn by the Sea in Cape Elizabeth, Maine, not only allows dogs, but they seem to welcome them with open arms. They have an extremely friendly pet policy that quite literally caters to canine guests. The inn has luxury one- and two-bedroom, ocean-view suites for guests who travel with their dogs. Beyond that, the canine vacationer will receive the same level of service as his human companion. The pet-friendly suites are furnished with amenities for the canine traveler.

Additionally, the Audubon Room prepares food especially for canine visitors including such things as doggie tapas and grilled range chicken with brown canine gravy. Dessert choices include Gourmet Doggy Bon Bons. Seasonal meals are geared for Thanksgiving, Christmas, and the Fourth of July. The pet menu is available from 7 A.M. to 10 P.M. They do have very reasonable safety guidelines in place for those who travel with their dog. The dog must be kept on leash when not in the suite. And you are asked to not leave your dog alone in the suite for any length of time because any dog will become lonely and cry when in a new environment. They also ask that you clean up after your dog when you walk him on the property. They require advance notice if you're traveling with a dog. With twenty-four-hour notification, they can provide pet walking. Their website provides some useful links for people traveling with a pet, along with their own doggie news section.

For information: innbythesea.com; e-mail: info@innbythesea.com; telephone (toll-free, outside Maine): 800-888-4287 or (local): 207-799-3134; fax: 207-799-4779; Inn by the Sea, 40 Bowery Beach Rd., Cape Elizabeth, ME 04107.

LOEWS HOTELS

"Loews loves pets," the hotel chain proudly proclaims. Upon check-in you'll receive a personal note from the general manager explaining the special pet services that are available for your four-legged traveling companion, including local walking routes, local groomers, veterinarians, pet attractions, and pet-friendly restaurants. Your companion will also find food and water bowls in the room, along with a placemat, toys, and treats. Pet room-service menus that were developed with a veterinarian are available. You'll also find a selection of dry and canned pet food.

The concierge can arrange dog-walking and pet-sitting services. And, as you would expect of a high-end hotel chain, they can also help with those "What did you forget?" items including dog beds, leashes, collars, pet toys, videos, and pooper scoopers. For more details, visit their website or see your travel agent.

For information: loewshotels.com.

STARWOOD HOTELS AND RESORTS

You probably know them best by their individual chain names including Westin, Sheraton, St. Regis, and W Hotels. Starwood has more than 740 properties in more than eighty countries. They probably have the most sweeping pet policy of any upscale hotel chain. Starwood has instituted a brandwide, dog-friendly program, the first in the hotel industry. Not just some of their properties accept dogs, *but all* do. In fact, they cater to canines with their Love That Dog (LTD) program. Your dog will be welcomed with a luxurious dog bed for his vacation slumbering pleasure. You'll also find amenities such as plush robes and leashes and collars at some Westin hotels.

The pet check-in package at W Hotels includes a dog toy, treat, and bone plus a special turn-down treat on the dog bed. Also at the five W Hotels in Manhattan, your four-legged traveling companion can get an in-room doggie massage by a licensed dog massage therapist. It's enough to make you wish you could be your own dog for awhile! Each brand-name hotel has a special signature dog bed; W has signature pillow-top beds, while Westin has Westin Heavenly Beds®, featuring a miniature Heavenly Bed duvet. W's bed is a colorful checkerboard pattern and Sheraton's dog beds are classic all-American red and blue design.

Each hotel brand also has food and water bowls and temporary ID tags with hotel contact information, which is both thoughtful and safety-conscious. Continuing to keep safety in mind, a traveling card—which contains safety tips for people traveling with their dogs—is provided upon check-in to all guests traveling with their dogs. The card is thanks to Starwood's partnership with the American Society for the Prevention of Cruelty to Animals (ASPCA).

For information: starwood.com.

Along with the upscale hotels, several motel chains often welcome canine visitors including **Four Seasons**, **Red Roof Inn**, **La Quinta**, **Howard Johnson**, **Days Inn**, **Travelodge**, **Super 8**, and **Motel 6**. Don't forget to say that you are traveling with a dog when you make your reservations, as policies can change from one hotel property to another, especially with independently owned hotels and motels. Some **Marriott** hotels are also pet-friendly.

INTERNATIONAL

COUNTRY HOLIDAYS

This company specializes in country cottages in England, Scotland, and Wales. They have a brochure as well as an Internet site. They have more than three thousand properties listed from cottages for two, to places that will sleep up to twenty-two. Many properties accept pets, which you can note as a requirement when searching their website so you can find the ones where your dog will be welcome. You are, however, asked to keep your dog off the furniture, exercise your dog outside in the garden, remove pet hairs from the carpets before you leave, and not leave your dog alone in the cottage.

All properties have been quality assessed using the English Tourism Council's grading system, and all properties are regularly inspected by a team of regional managers. They also feature midweek breaks for those who can't manage to get away for an entire week. Midweek breaks are less expensive than weekend breaks because the four-night break is priced the same as the three-night weekend.

The website offers you a virtual tour around one of the cottages and you can do a currency exchange so you have a better idea of the cost if you live outside the United Kingdom. They also offer a selection of cottages in Ireland and France. Not only do they prepare your accommodation, but they will supply you with directions for getting there. Cottages are cleaned between visitors so you'll only need to unpack once you arrive. The only extra charge for cleaning would be if you have left it in such condition that it needs more than regular cleaning. A local guide to events and sightseeing options will be at the property so you can tailor your vacation to your individual interests. More details of the company and their properties can be found at their website, where you can register for a free newsletter. They also have a handy glossary of terms to help you understand local expressions if you're traveling from the United Kingdom along with a list of abbreviations used to help you understand property descriptions.

For information: country-holidays.co.uk; e-mail: ch.enquiry@holiday cottagesgroup.com; telephone: +44 08700 781200; Cottage Holidays, Spring Mill, Earby, Barnoldswick, Lancashire BB94 0AA, United Kingdom.

PETS 'N' PEOPLE HOLIDAYS—MULLUMBIMBY COTTAGE

Well-mannered dogs are welcome with their human companions at this holiday destination in Australia, only fifteen minutes from Byron

Bay. They have a fenced backyard, and dogs are welcome to play in the garden. Even dog sitting is available. And they promise dog-exercise areas and dog-friendly places a short drive away in Byron Shire. And a dog-friendly beach and Brunswick Heads is only seven minutes away. *For information:* bigvolcano.com.au/custom/pets/index.html; e-mail: joyvogel437@yahoo.com; telephone: (02) 6684 2522 or (international): 61-2-6684 2522 or (mobile): 0439 330 259; fax (02) 6684 6443 or (international): 61-2-6684 6443; Joy Vogel, Mullumbimby Cottage, P.O. Box 1262, Byron Bay N.S.W., 2481, Australia.

PET-TRAVEL-RELATED WEBSITES
While books on traveling with your dog are available at virtually any bookstore, many websites are dedicated to the topic, and they have amazingly comprehensive lists of hotels and motels that will welcome your dog. Some are specific to one area, some are countrywide. Here are a few to browse at your leisure.

ALLSTAYS
While not specifically a pet site, AllStays has a special section for people who travel with their pet. One special feature of this website is that you can locate pet-friendly accommodations on every continent and in ten languages. They are also donating 1 percent of all online bookings at AllStays to the aid of animals. Their instruction for finding a pet-friendly place is to look for the "P" next to the listing, however, they candidly inform site users that they should check with the hotel when booking because management changes can occur as can changes to their pet policy.
For information: allstays.com/special/petfriendly.htm.

BRING YOUR PET
Bringyourpet.com boasts that they offer only the highest quality pet-friendly lodging in the United States. Their user-friendly site allows you to click on any state on the map featured on the home page to find lodging. The menu on the side lists helpful pages, including pet etiquette geared to travel; travel tips, including things to remember to

pack for your pet; events throughout the country; and emergencies. You can also sign up for a free newsletter.

For information: bringyourpet.com.

PETS ON THE GO

Pets on the Go lists more than eighteen thousand pet-friendly hotels and chains. The site also has a vast array of resources including travel tips, shopping, sightseeing, pet-friendly events, and emergency advice. Pets on the Go is reportedly the top recommended accommodation resource by the Humane Society of the United States. The site also has a message board available where pet owners can ask questions. Be aware that some features on the site, such as the events page and the message board, can only be accessed by joining the site. Membership is $14.95 per year. They keep track of discounted hotel rates for members and have an enriched database for members to search. Members also are able to access savings on travel-related items.

For information: petsonthego.com/index.htm.

INTERNATIONAL

LE DOG STOP

This website provides one place to go for both travel and pet relocation. They also feature the Pet Travel Scheme, which allows dogs to travel to some European countries without having to be quarantined; information about moving your pet internationally; as well as information and advice regarding the quarantine process and your options, which include the site owner's boarding facility, Cani-Excel. Renee Hemming, the website's owner, is a U.K. qualified veterinary nurse and a former RSPCA kennel manager. Pet health insurance information is also on the site, as well as pet-friendly accommodations in Europe, and they even have an e-mail forum for any pet owner who travels with their pets. Le Dog Stop is a member of Independent Pet and Animal Transportation Association (IPATA).

For information: ledogstop.com; e-mail: info@ledogstop.com.

PET FRIENDLY CANADA

This is a website filled with pet-friendly lodgings throughout Canada. You can select the province that interests you and click on it to find a list for that area. The site includes Prince Edward Island, Nova Scotia, and Newfoundland as well as the Yukon and Northwest Territories. There's also a link for places in the United States as well as one for vacation properties that are for sale. Pet Friendly Canada also has a travel checklist, a list of frequently asked questions, a link for pet supplies, a free newsletter, and links to pet-related websites. The travel listings include everything from hotels to cottages, cabins, and bed and breakfasts that will welcome you and your pet. You can also sign up for their free monthly newsletter. The website also has a thoughtful reminder to please spay or neuter your pet.

For information: petfriendly.ca; e-mail (for general inquiries): info@ petfriendly.com (other specific e-mail addresses for the website are online); telephone: 403-226-6668 (Phone hours are Monday through Friday, 10 A.M. to 5 P.M., MST.); Pet Friendly Canada, Internet Inquiries, 111 Panorama Hills Pl. N.W., Calgary, AB, T3K 4R9, Canada.

6

Art and Photos

H aving a portrait of your dog is something that you will enjoy for the rest of your life. You may choose to have yourself photographed with your dog or have your dog photographed alone. Or, perhaps, you will choose to have a portrait painted in oils or pastels or drawn in charcoal. Whichever you choose, many very talented canine artists and photographers can capture your dog's spirit and personality. Prices, of course, will vary.

ARTWORK

Dog people enjoy portraits of dogs in the breed that they own. Even more special is a portrait of your own dog, a lasting memory that captures the essence of a beloved family member. That portrait can be done in a variety of mediums from oil paintings and watercolors to sculpture and more.

TERRY ALBERT

Artist Terry Albert specializes in portraits of your pet, but she also has a line of note cards featuring various breeds and prints of Labrador

Retriever puppies for sale. Working in watercolor, a difficult medium but one in which she has amazing control, she carefully creates each portrait using both watercolor and colored pencil. To create an original portrait, the owner provides snapshots that she can use as a guide along with instructions. The snapshots are returned with the finished painting. She also contacts the owner to discuss the portrait before beginning work on it. She chooses a good pose from among the snapshot photos, then uses the other photos to help her fill in whatever is missing. She prefers close-up photos and suggests that the owner get down on the dog's level and photograph him or her straight on, instead of looking down at the dog.

She does two types of portraits: a head or full-body study with no background, or a head or full-body study with the background of your choice. She offers ideas and also suggests that people browse the galleries on her website for inspiration. She can also do a multiple pet portrait or a larger size. Satisfaction is guaranteed. She will either fix what you don't like or take it back and refund your money. You can see a wide range of portraits at her website. She also does wonderful name T-shirts with the breed name surrounded by dogs of that breed, but they are for group orders only and must be special ordered and would probably appeal to clubs or for special events.

For information: terryalbert.com; e-mail: terryalbert@cox.net; Terry Albert, 17087 W. Bernardo Dr., #105, San Diego, CA 92127.

ROD ARBOGAST

Pet and wildlife artist Rod Arbogast has a bachelor of fine arts degree and can be commissioned to create a portrait of your dog. Or, you can buy one of his prints if he has something in your special breed. He also has some of his original artwork for sale. He paints in watercolor and has tremendous control of that difficult medium. He believes that watercolor allows him to show subtleties in the dog's coat color and texture. He is also able to capture the dog's personality and expression.

For information: rodarbogast.com; e-mail: rpaartist@aol.com or rod arbogast@enter.net; telephone: 610-432-0771; Rod Arbogast, 1629 W. Pennsylvania St., Allentown, PA 18102.

BETH BLOCH CREATIVE CARDS

Beth Bloch's amusing cards combine her photographs of her dog, Bella, with her watercolor painting to create whimsical cards for nearly every occasion. She prints the cards on recycled paper using soy-based inks. She has greeting cards, enclosure cards, magnets, invitations, holiday cards, gift tags, as well as custom cards. Your pet's photo can be used to create a truly individual card, such as greetings cards, party invitations, moving cards, or a personalized print to frame and hang on your wall. She will need one to three photographs of your dog (or cat, or other loved one) that are well focused, clean, and free of scratches and smudges. The photos will be returned. Alternately, you can send high-resolution, jpeg images via e-mail. Backgrounds will be dropped out as Beth Bloch creates a watercolor painting to serve as an individual background for your card.

There is an additional charge for each additional pet or human in a single portrait, which covers the cost of cleaning and scanning each photo. Further instructions are on her website. Full payment is required in advance for all orders; shipping is additional. Orders are shipped within three weeks. Beth Bloch Creative Cards retains the reproduction rights on your artwork, and you may not use it for commercial purposes.

For information: bbcreativecards.com; e-mail: bethart@mind.net; telephone and fax: 541-488-1197; Creative Cards, 401 Taylor St., Ashland, OR 97520.

RON BURNS

Ron Burns's bright and eye-catching dog portraits capture the dog in a rather different manner. The bright colors that characterized Andy Warhol's work also leap from Ron Burns's canvases. His career began as a graphic designer, a more conservative art form. Starting with portraits of his own pets, he quickly found his niche when he took photos of homeless pets at a shelter and painted a series of portraits for an art show in Los Angeles. He sent a portion of the sales proceeds to the shelter, which is something he continues to do. He donates part of the proceeds from his work to animal welfare organizations. Burns soon learned that it would be impossible to work with thousands of individual shelters, so he now works with two specific charities and corporate groups to raise awareness through programs that benefit animal shelters.

Signed and numbered, limited-edition prints are available at his website, along with commemorative prints, which are prints of portraits the artist has donated to a nonprofit organization to help raise awareness and funds. He also has a book of his paintings for sale, and you can purchase original artwork or commission him to do a portrait of your special companion. He begins each painting with the eyes, capturing the dog's personality. He believes the colors he chooses also reflect the animal's personality.

You can sign up for his newsletter at the website. Ron Burns is the first and only artist in residence for the Humane Society of the United States and was the official artist for the American Society for the Prevention of Cruelty to Animals' Adopt a Shelter Dog Month in 2001 and 2002. On November 11, 2000, the mayor and city council of Fort Lauderdale, Florida, proclaimed Ron Burns Day to honor his contributions to companion animals.

For information: ronburns.com; e-mail: rufus@ronburns.com.

CRAZY DOG LADY CUSTOM PET PORTRAIT QUILTS

Jan Queijo, the self-proclaimed "crazy dog lady," can create a custom portrait of your dog (or other pet) in a quilt wall hanging. She creates it using a clear photo that you provide. (The photo will be returned.) It takes just a few weeks to complete. It is made of appliquéd individual pieces of appropriate-colored fabric to depict the different areas of your pet, and then she embroiders details such as eyes, nose, mouth, stripes, or spots, and so forth. She also has premade pieces for sale at her website. You can also visit the gallery section of her website to see samples of her recent work. If you would like a memorial quilt of a deceased pet, it can be made with wings and a halo. Your custom-made quilt can also be personalized with your pet's name hand embroidered on it. You choose the quilt size as well as the colors of the fabrics. Fifty percent of payment is required in advance.

Queijo has worked as an animal control officer, a volunteer coordinator at her local animal shelter, director of another animal shelter, a pet sitter, and a receptionist at her local animal hospital. Initial contact with her can be made via e-mail. Or you can use the inquiry page on her website.

For information: crazydoglady.com; e-mail: jan@crazydoglady.com.

CREATIVE WOODWORKS BY MARTY

This is probably one of the most unusual and interesting vendors at dog shows. Her dogs (and cats) are beautifully handcrafted and come in an array of products. You can also have something custom made from your photo for an additional charge. The animal is cut from thin wood, hand painted, and applied to one of her products for a three-dimensional effect. Products include wood jewelry, silver jewelry, welcome signs, baskets in various styles, storage chests (22″ by 13″ by 11″), large and small oval plaques with stands, pocketbooks, and framed pictures. All of the designs are hand cut and painted by Marty Gordon. Marty can be found at various dog shows in New England or you can visit her website to order.

For information: creativedogwood.com; e-mail: marty@creativedog wood.com; telephone: 860-645-6678; Creative Woodworks by Marty Gordon, 424 Hackmatack St., Manchester, CT 06040.

DANNYQUEST DESIGNS

Dannyquest Designs features the artwork of sculptor Tony Acevdo, who is senior design artist for this company. His sculptures are included in the permanent collection of the AKC Museum of the Dog, and his work is offered as best in show, challenge, and memorial trophies at dog shows around the world.

Dannyquest Designs has been producing an American-made collection of handcrafted dog sculpture for almost forty years. The growing collection comes in more than 125 breeds of dogs in miniatures to huge display pieces. From the whimsical to the historical, the collection includes rare breeds and popular ones, and each sculpture is carefully crafted to represent the best specimens of each breed. New artwork is being added almost weekly. And, lamps and bookends are now available. More than two thousand pieces and more than a thousand photos can be found in their online catalog. You can e-mail a request for a minicatalog including the breed(s) of your choice. Dannyquest can also be found at select dog shows. Custom designs of dog-breed sculptures are available as well. The sculptures can depict special scenes or they can create life-size reproductions in cold cast or foundry bronze.

For information: dannyquest.com; e-mail: dannyquest@aol.com; telephone: 714-891-4121.

DREAMSCAPE CANINE COLLECTIBLES

Dreamscape Canine Collectibles includes artists working in different mediums, portrait artists, D.L. Engle Bronzes, and more. Dreamscape can be accessed on the Web, or you can see them at a few dog shows. They have limited and open-edition, fine-art prints as well as original dog paintings. The bronzes, miniatures just two or three inches tall, are limited edition, and they are gift items. Dreamscape is adding artists, so you can check back at the website to see what's new and you can be added to their mailing list. They also have a list of breeds available and you can see what is available in your special breed. They feature T-shirts, mugs, and mouse pads with humorous illustrations by Angi Laframboise. Some depict dog sports such as agility, flyball, and obedience as well as holiday designs.

Artist Cindy Brassfield paints original oil portraits on canvas. You can see samples of her work at the website, along with prices, and commission a portrait. Artist Dawn Secord paints in oils and watercolors, but her favorite medium is pastels. She, too, can be commissioned to paint a portrait of your dog. Samples and prices are at the website. And the site has original watercolor and pencil portraits by Heidi Choquette. Dreamscape has a dog rescue fund-raising program.

For information: dreamscapek9.com; e-mail: priggins@dreamscapek9.com; telephone: 404-606-2152 or (to order): 770-942-5419; fax: 770-489-9371; Dreamscape Canine Collectibles, 4269 Leola Rd., Douglasville, GA 30135.

CATE AND ANNIE FITT JEWELRY

The Fitt Sisters create jewelry and miniatures of dogs as well as horses and other animals. They create their jewelry in different styles and feature vintage dog-tag jewelry and treasure necklaces. They were inspired by historical portrait jewelry, and Annie's painting is combined with Cate's fine jewelry design. They have pieces for sale and can also be commissioned to create a special portrait of your specific dog. Commissioned pieces are an additional $100. Gold or vermeil (gilded silver) is available by request and it's priced by the market value. More than fifty breeds of dogs and horses are represented in their hand-crafted jewelry. They also make jewelry incorporating antique and hunt-club buttons without altering or damaging the buttons. They specialize in jewelry for the fancier and the jewelry collector, as well as miniature portraits commissions. They have received a number of awards including the Art Show at the Dog Show. You can see their work online along with a list of events where you can find them.

For information: fittsisters.com/generic11.html; e-mail: daylilly@erols .com; telephone (toll-free): 888-353-5348; Cate and Annie Fitt Jewelry, P.O. Box 5322, Richmond, VA 23220.

ROBIN GARCIA

Robin Garcia's fine-art gallery showcases dog prints, mainly Sight-hounds, although you'll also find Parson Russell Terriers, Cavalier King Charles Spaniels, Great Danes, and Golden Retrievers. They also offer jewelry for sale, and they sell therapy neck wraps for stress relief. The wraps are filled with a natural seed and can be heated in the microwave for no more than two minutes. The wraps can also be used as cold packs by chilling in the freezer.

And don't forget to check out their handcrafted puppet dolls. Sighthounds are predominantly featured in the work, which is logical since the artist, Robin Garcia, breeds Saluki and Scottish Deerhounds. Garcia studied art at the Chicago Art Institute, Northern Illinois University, and the University of California, San Diego. She has illustrated professionally for thirty years.

Of particular interest on the website are the limited ParkPupPets. These precious hand and finger puppets were designed and hand-crafted by Robin Garcia; the heads were made into limited molds, cast in resin, and hand painted. The female dogs wear a reversible dress and the males wear a reversible vest. Each PupPet is unique and comes with its own pedigree. Each is sold as a "limited litter" and signed by the "breeder" or artist. Only forty puppets were created, ten of each: Golden, Great Dane, Parson Russell, and LongDog. You'll have to specify breed and sex when you order, but only a few remain. According to Garcia, if you're not completely thrilled with your order, you can return it to her for a full refund.

For information: telephone: 760-749-5382; Robin Garcia, 30964 Cole Grade Rd., Valley Center, CA 92082.

MARY JUNG IVY ORIGINALS

Mary Jung is a Bull Terrier owner whose artwork encompasses all breeds and is represented by both wonderful breed studies and whimsical caricatures. She has had a variety of animals throughout her life including an Appaloosa horse. She has owned German Shepherds and Giant Schnauzers. She works in oil and watercolor–colored pencil. She currently does some wonderful pieces in porcelain in all breeds. China painting is an old art form that can be traced back to ancient China and Persia. China paint is transparent and is applied in light layers, firing it in a kiln to fuse the paint with the glaze of the porcelain.

Mary Jung will accept commissions to do a one-of-a-kind porcelain collector's piece of your dog. She can also do it on a porcelain tile. You can see her Bull Terrier designs on giftware such as jewelry boxes, cookie canisters, rubber stamps, mugs, Christmas ornaments, and limited edition prints at her website, but she will also do them in the breed of your choice. You can commission her to do a portrait of your dog (any breed). And she does custom-made brooches. Her artwork has been featured in a number of books, including *The Angell Memorial Animal Hospital Book of Wellness and Preventive Care for Dogs*. Her illustrations have also been featured in magazines and she has won two coveted Maxwell Awards from the Dog Writers' Association of America, Inc., for her illustrations. Her artwork has won a number of other awards and one of her painted China plates is in the permanent collection of the Museum of the Dog. To find Mary Jung's Ivy Originals on the Web visit either website that follows.

For information: jarroguebullterriers.net (scroll down to The Bully Shoppe) or btshoppingmall.com; e-mail: btart@aol.com.

NANCY ROSS

Nancy Ross's pet portraits capture the personality as well as the physical characteristics of the dog. A Pekingese breeder, she has a special affinity for coats with an ability that seems to capture each individual strand of hair. She works in pastel or pen and ink—the choice is yours. She also does note cards, shirts, and mouse pads depicting charming Pekingese in a variety of poses that will attract even those who don't own a Peke. She also does a Pekingese holiday card each year.

For information: lindyg.com/nanross; e-mail: pekeart@earthlink.net; telephone: 718-331-9523; Nancy Ross, 1559 82nd St., Brooklyn, NY 11228.

WILLIAM SECORD GALLERY

This absolutely marvelous art gallery on Manhattan's Upper East Side specializes in exhibiting and selling fine nineteenth- and twentieth-century paintings, works on paper, and collectibles, as well as books, each with dogs as its subject. The gallery owner, William Secord, was the founding director of the Museum of the Dog. But, when the museum was moved to St. Louis in 1990, he decided to stay in New York and open his own gallery. This is the only gallery of its kind. Paintings are beautifully displayed as you move from room to room. Paintings and prints in the Yellow Room are hung floor to ceiling in the Victorian style, making it a room in which you will want to spend extra time. Their website is well worth visiting on a regular basis because it's updated with new items weekly. Current exhibitions can be viewed online, and you can do a search of inventory along with specific categories, such as nineteenth- or twentieth-century works, or you can commission a painting, fine prints, and collectibles. You can commission any one of three artists through the Secord Gallery: Barrie Barnett, Christine Merrill, or Charlotte Sorre. William Secord is considered the world authority on the dog in art and is the author of *Dog Painting, 1840–1940: A Social History of the Dog in Art*, as well as *Dog Painting: The European Breeds*, both of which are available at the gallery and online, as are some select other books. Online, you'll also find a link to the breed of the month. A visit to the gallery not only brings a delight of painted images by such artists as Edwin Landseer and Maud Earl, but terra-cottas, dog collars, porcelains, and selected rare books on dogs. Twentieth-century artists such as printmaker Bert Cobb and the drawings of Gladys Emerson Cook are among the gallery's delights. The William Secord Gallery has more recently branched out to the contemporary market with the gallery now representing both Barrie Barnett and Christine Merrill.

For information: dogpainting.com; e-mail: wsecord@dogpainting .com; telephone (toll-free in North America): 877-249-DOGS or (local): 212-249-0075; fax: 212-288-1938; The William Secord Gallery, Inc., 52 East 76th St., New York, NY 10021.

GLORIA VOSS

Art by Gloria Voss features the artist's hand-painted sweatshirts. Voss's slogan, "Artwear items that are fun to wear," really captures the essence of her work. She will custom paint a shirt using a picture of your dog or dogs. Prices vary, depending upon the style shirt you choose. If ordering more than just a head study on the shirt, Voss will want some guidance regarding layout and whether you want one or more dogs featured. The more photos she has, the better. Often, the shirt will incorporate a dog sport in which the owner and dog are involved. She also does more generic sweatshirts and T-shirts featuring her own designs such as Gotta Dance Freestyle and Therapy Dog, among others. She also has canvas tote bags and she makes handcrafted jewelry. *For information:* ejourney.com/~gloriavossart; e-mail: gnsvoss@ ejourney.com; telephone: 989-426-2841; Gloria Voss, 3323 E. Pinecrest Dr., Gladwin, MI 48624.

INTERNATIONAL

DEIRDRE ASHDOWN

Artist Deirdre Ashdown, whose illustrations have appeared in books and more, has a variety of products available featuring her work, or she can be commissioned to do a portrait of your special dog. She has prints; greeting cards; an assortment of gift items, including pen stands and letter openers; as well as jewelry, including broaches and lockets. She works mainly in Indian ink and colored inks. Indian ink is permanent, not affected by light, and is ideally suited to her very detailed and fine line drawings. She does portraits of cats as well as dogs, and her portraits also contain flowers, bees, butterflies, or seashells, which not only add interest, but give the dog or cat something on which they can focus.

All of her original artwork is individually priced and will vary according to the estimated time it will take to complete the drawing. A firm price is given when the commission is agreed upon and won't increase even if it takes longer to complete than the original estimate. She prefers to work using several good-quality photographs of the dog or cat so that she can both capture the correct color and markings of the animal as well as his or her individual personality, which means that a good head study photo should be included. Photographs don't have to be professional but should be clear enough to allow her to see the correct coat color. She endeavors to portray the animal at his best and is familiar with most breed standards. She can minimize faults and emphasize virtues, add or take away coat, darken eyes, and bring the dog up on his pasterns if it's necessary, making the dog look his best. Or she can draw the dog as he or she is, depending upon the request. For further information or for a no-obligation quote, you can write, telephone, or fax Ms. Ashdown.

For information: nouveau.fsnet.co.uk; e-mail: nouveau@papillons 60.freeserve.co.uk; telephone and fax: 0171 739 7429; Deirdre Ashdown, 43 Dunmore Point, Virginia Gardens, Gascoigne Place, London E2 7 LX, United Kingdom. In the U.S. or Canada, customers can order directly from her agent in the United States: e-mail: davidswoodets@

yahoo.com; telephone: 707-792-4344; Cheryl Abbott, 459 Ava Ave., Rohnert Park, CA 94928.

BOX TREE COTTAGE DESIGNS

Ann Griffiths's artistry takes a different turn from most. She creates cross-stitch and tapestry (needlepoint) charts. Aside from the collection that she sells, you can also commission her to create a cross-stitch or needlepoint chart of your dog from your photograph. It includes a color chart and symbol chart as well as details of the threads you'll need to create your cross-stitch or needlepoint portrait of your dog. You specify whether you want needlepoint or cross-stitch and the size you want. You don't pay until you're happy with the design. You can view samples on the Box Tree Cottage Designs website. You will have to obtain a specific quote for the cost of an individual cross-stitch or needlepoint chart and it will remain exclusively yours, a one-of-a-kind creation. Ann Griffiths also creates cross-stitch and tapestry charts of cats, wedding samplers, flowers, and much more.

For information: gingercat.ltd.uk/boxtreecot; e-mail: agriffi381@aol .com; telephone and fax: 01905 381506 (From the United States replace the leading "0" with "01144."); Ann Griffiths, Box Tree Cottage Designs, Libbery, Grafton Flyford, Worcestershire, WR7 4PE, United Kingdom.

PAULINE GLEDHILL

Animal portraiture is the work of Pauline Gledhill. Her mediums are watercolor and pencil drawing. She uses your photograph of your dog (or horse or cat) as her guide in creating the portrait and really captures the animal's personality. After four years in art school studying graphic art and illustration, she turned to her first love—animal portraits. She uses watercolor and gouache to give a delicate and detailed feeling to the picture. She also works with graphite and colored pencils.

You can see an example of a photograph and the finished portrait on her website. You'll also find prints for sale and you can commission her to do a portrait of your special companion. If you opt for that, you will be asked to supply as many clear photographs as you can, prefer-ably taken at eye level with the animal. While she prefers photographs, she can also work from a digital image sent via e-mail. She asks that you identify the photos you want her to use in the final portrait as well as the ones that best match the dog's color. More details are at her web-site. All photos will be returned with the finished portrait. All work is mounted but unframed and it takes from two to six weeks to receive your portrait, depending upon the time of year and your location. A 50 percent deposit is required when you order, with the balance due when the portrait is finished. You can arrange to see a preview of the finished portrait via e-mail before it's sent to you. At the website you'll find prices quoted in both British pounds and U.S. dollars. She offers a money-back guarantee if you're not satisfied and you return the por-trait within fourteen days of receiving it.

For information: yourpetpics.co.uk; e-mail: pauline@yourpetpics .co.uk; Pauline Gledhill, 424 Northenden Rd., Sale, Cheshire, M33 2PR, United Kingdom.

PETS IN PASTEL

Pets in Pastel is the artistry of Sarah Theophilus, who sold her first commissioned portrait when she was only sixteen. She was born in the United Kingdom, moved to Canada as a child. She has had a career as a Web designer but now paints full-time and her portraits have appeared on magazine covers. She's a member of the AKC Museum of the Dog Artists' Registry, Oil Pastel Association International, and The League of Animal Artists. Theophilus creates oil pastel pet portraits of dogs, cats, and horses using photographs (which will be safely returned) to guide her in creating a lifelike image of the pet. (If the photographs were professionally taken, you will need the photogra-pher's permission to use them as the basis for the portrait.) While she's creating the portrait, she sends images of it to you so she can receive feedback.

Portrait prices are on the website along with an inquiry form and no deposit is required. Portraits can be any size and are on high-quality, acid-free, cold-pressed paper stock. The finished painting is sprayed with a fixative so it will be safe and have a long life. The amount of time it takes to complete a portrait depends upon the number of commissions she has at the time. She usually has a six- to nine-month wait list, and she accepts Christmas orders up to a year in advance. She will, however, try to have a portrait ready in time for a special date to commemorate a special occasion.

Her website includes photography tips, and she is always adding new portraits. Theophilus offers free e-cards that you can create using a selection of the artist's portraits. She also has art prints and cards. The website can also be translated into French, German, Italian, Portuguese, and Spanish.

For information: petsinpastel.com; e-mail: portraits@petsinpastel.com; Pets in Pastel, Chatterton Way, Victoria, BC V8X 5H7, Canada.

RUDISNAPS

This U.K. company takes a photograph of your dog, transfers it to canvas or paper, and then paints it, creating a rather unusual portrait with a very contemporary look. You can obtain a portrait in one of three ways. You could bring your dog to their trade stand at one of the dog shows the company attends in the United Kingdom. Or, you could send a favorite photo (of course this is subject to its suitability to be turned into a portrait). Or, they could assign one of their photographers to travel to your home if you live in the mainland United Kingdom. Portraits are available in four sizes: 24 cm by 30 cm, 30 cm by 40 cm, 40 cm by 50 cm, or 50 cm by 70 cm. The portrait is done in acrylic and can be finished on either canvas or paper, and it will be framed to your specifications.

For information: rudisnaps.co.uk; e-mail: sales@rudisnaps.co.uk.

SIMPLY FINE ART

Simply Fine Art was established to publish limited-edition prints by British artist Stuart J. Mallard, whose canine studies are striking. More than thirty breeds have been featured with more on the way. Many prints are or are close to being sold out. In addition to being a wildlife artist, Mallard is involved in the dog fancy as an international dog show judge, which has inspired his canine art.

For information: dogtown.co.uk/simplyfineart; e-mail: simplyfineart@ onetel.net.uk; telephone: 44(0) 1909 722141 noting U.K. time to have your order completed by telephone if you prefer not to send credit card information via the Internet; fax: 44(0) 1909 724121.

PHOTOGRAPHERS

MARY BLOOM

Mary Bloom is the official photographer of the North Shore Animal League, the world's largest animal adoption agency. She has also traveled to overseas dog shows, including Crufts, on assignment for dog publications. An award-winning photographer, Mary Bloom has a knack for capturing the essential quality of the dog. She loves dogs of all sizes, colors, ages, and breeds and it shows in her work. She admits that she loves photographing dogs as members of the family, dogs with seniors, and service dogs. "My goal is to teach the world how important dogs are in our lives and how they help make a better world." Mary Bloom will travel to your home or facility to capture the dog and its people in its own environment.

For information: e-mail: bloomdog@ulster.net; telephone: 845-758-9109; Mary Bloom, 192 Yantz Rd., Red Hook, NY 12571.

LISA CROFT-ELLIOTT

Lisa Croft-Elliott is an award-winning photographer, journalist, and owner/handler who exhibits Toy and Miniature Poodles. She photographs dogs both at shows and in more natural settings at home or in the kennel. She claims that she doesn't understand people but she does understand dogs: what they are thinking, what they love, and how they behave. She says this gives her a decided edge in capturing the real essence of the canine in her lens. In pursuit of all things canine, Croft-Elliott travels the world covering the top show dogs in their careers. Her photographic essays and articles frequently appear in publications in Japan, England, France, the United States, and Canada. She will travel anywhere to photograph dogs. She has three websites devoted to her work.

For information: wickedkewl.com, dogphotographer.com, or dogpress .co.uk; e-mail: dogphotographer@aol.com; telephone: 401-821-0505 or (mobile): 401-996-2056; Lisa Croft-Elliott, 22 Reservoir Rd., Coventry, RI 02816.

JIM DRATFIELD'S PETOGRAPHY™

Inspired by his own dog, the late Kuma, Jim Dratfield has photographed the dogs of the rich and famous, including Henry Kissinger, Jennifer Aniston, Bebe Neuwirth, and Laura Dern. He travels extensively, photographing dogs for those who want a Dratfield photographic portrait of their companion. Along with photographic portraits, Petography also offers an interesting line of items to complement the photographs; each can have your dog's portrait on it. These items include cufflinks designed by jeweler Laura Graham, custom handcrafted photo albums designed by Kristin Olson, and other items including briefcase business card holder, photo boxes, framed desk portrait, and jewelry. He also has both handmade and commercial note cards. You can request more information or a brochure by writing, e-mailing, or calling. A look at his website will give you a view of his work, which also includes having published several books of his photography.

For information: petography.com; e-mail: petography@aol.com; telephone and fax: 212-245-0914; Petography, Inc., 25 Central Park West, Suite 3A, New York, NY 10023.

DOGPATCH PHOTOGRAPHY

Dogpatch Photography is owned by Mary Jo Sminkey, who has been taking action shots of dog sports for more than a dozen years. Competing in dog sports for more than fifteen years has given her a real feel for photographing the activities and capturing those special moments. Sminkey uses a digital camera with a professional lens to get those special moments and allow for a wide range of prints and products with your special dog(s) on them. She has also created a screensaver sold through cleanrun.com. Mary Jo can be booked for your special dog events.

For information: dogpatchphoto.com; e-mail: maryjo@dogpatchphoto .com; telephone: 703-709-0795; Dogpatch Photography, 415 Florida Ave., Herndon, VA 20170.

DOGPHOTO

Kerrin Winter and Dale Churchill are a husband-and-wife team of dog photographers who work together to create what they call "quintessential" breed images of show dogs. They will do a variety of poses including free-stacked shots, head shots, shots of the dog gaiting, as well as photos with and without the handler in a variety of locales. When they met, he was photographing fashion models while she was photographing dogs and horses. They combined their talents and now travel the country photographing dogs and will meet you anywhere in the United States for your photographing adventure.

They have a variety of images that they hand place on a range of products available on their website. They cannot put a kennel name on one of their products with one of their stock shots, because that might imply that the dog pictured was of that kennel's breeding. They provide merchandise to a few rescue groups at a 50 percent discount, which is their cost plus or minus a few pennies. They offer their products to retailers at a 30 percent discount. In both cases, there is a minimum order. Details are at their website.

Their online store has shirts, magnets, auto license tags, crate tags, and more. If you are not satisfied with the quality of any item they deliver, let them know by e-mail within three days and they'll provide a return address. You must, of course, return the item unused and they'll either, at your choice, issue a refund to your credit card or send a replacement. They also have a link to play their jigsaw puzzles online and another link leading to their free desktop photos for Windows PC users.

For information: dogphoto.com; e-mail: dale@dogphoto.com or kerrin@dogphoto.com; telephone: 586-530-0309.

SHEL SECUNDA

Shel Secunda is a gifted photographer whose work has been featured in fashion supplements for the *New York Times* as well as in the permanent collection of the International Center of Photography in New York City. His work has also been exhibited in museums and galleries throughout the United States and Europe. He has extensive experience as a photojournalist and fashion and fine art photographer. His portraits of well-known celebrities such as Meryl Streep, Barbara Walters, and Carol Burnett have graced the covers and appeared in the pages of national magazines such as *New York*, *TV Guide*, *Life*, and *Ladies' Home Journal*. Five books of Secunda's photographs have been published, including *The Bond: People and Their Animals*, which features photos of notables like Mary Tyler Moore, James Earl Jones, and Morley Safer. He brings that wealth of experience and creativity to his pet portraits, which can also be done with human family members included in the photograph. He is available to travel the world.

For information: shelsecundaphotography.com; e-mail: info@shel secundaphotography.com; telephone: 203-431-1931; Shel Secunda, 5 Hawthorne Hill Rd., Ridgefield, CT 06877.

ALICE SU

Alice Su specializes in canine portraiture, aiming to capture the essence of the individual dog, ". . . so that she or he stands out from scores of others of the same breed, color, and sex. My highest compliments from dog owners are, invariably, remarks such as, 'That's Max!' 'You've definitely got him,' or of course, ecstatic screams and gasps of recognition." She will travel anywhere in the United States to photograph your dog, taking cameras, lights, and backdrops where necessary. She has a nearly inexhaustible supply of patience and will spend as much time as necessary to ensure satisfaction. Her photographs have appeared on many magazine and book covers and complete calendars of her work have been published.

For information: alicesuphotography; e-mail: tefnut@earthlink.net; telephone: 212-477-0977; fax: 212-460-9306; Alice Su, 321 East 22nd St. #4E, New York, NY 10010.

TONI TUCKER

Toni Tucker's photography has an almost lyrical quality to it and her photos grace the book *Zen Dogs*. She captures a mood with each photograph. A wonderful variety can be seen in her line of greeting cards available on her website. All of the photographs on her website are for sale. She also has an extensive stock library of breed images. You can book a private portrait session. E-mail or phone to obtain fees or prices for the greeting cards and photos at her website.

For information: tonitucker.com; e-mail: tuckerstudio@earthlink.net; telephone: 860-364-0004; Tucker Photographer, LLC, 6 Herb Rd., Sharon, CT 06069.

TINA VALANT

Boca Raton, Florida, photographer Tina Valant has an assortment of items that you can have customized with a photo from Tina's gallery, including T-shirts, mouse pads, totes, and mugs. She photographs events free of charge and then collects everyone's e-mail address, posts the pictures to a gallery at her website, and then prints are available to order, along with enlargements or special items featuring the selected image. Valant will also photograph you and your special companion (or just your dog alone) by appointment. She charges by the roll; the client gets their 4″ by 6″ proofs to keep and reprints, enlargements, and/or items featuring the selected portrait can be ordered. She travels throughout Florida and says that she has a "unique understanding and camaraderie with animals, domestic and wild. This is reflected in my photography."

For information: http://tinavalant.com; e-mail: tvalant@aol.com; telephone (mobile): 561-945-6363.

7

Training and Day Care

The world of dog training is moving forward quite rapidly, away from aversive training and toward positive training. This is good news for dogs and their owners, as a positive relationship can only strengthen the human-animal bond. The movement appears to be universal, since it is indeed spanning the globe.

Beyond strengthening the bond, training also makes your dog a companion who is even more fun to be with and is welcomed in more places because of his good behavior. Training will also make your dog more confident. And sharing in various activities means that your dog is less likely to develop bad habits. A dog who is confident that his owner will share time with him, and not leave him in the backyard and ignore him, is happier and more secure.

Dog trainers are not licensed and although there is no standardization, organizations are available for trainers to join. Membership alone, however, does not guarantee anything. As a consumer, you should be as careful when you select a dog trainer as you would when you choose a coach for your child. When looking for a trainer, ask to observe a class. Never make your dog do anything that makes you uncomfortable. If it seems wrong or harsh, don't be afraid to refuse.

The newest and best training methods are positive. Happily for you and your dog, aversive training is quickly becoming a thing of the past.

GENERAL TRAINING

You can find a number of organizations around the world for dog-obedience trainers. This is a good, general place to start if you're looking for a teacher for your dog. It will be up to you to decide if the individual trainer is right for you and your dog, but the organizations should be able to provide names and contact information for dog trainers in your area.

ASSOCIATION OF PET DOG TRAINERS (APDT)

The APDT in the United States (there are similar, but separate, organizations in other countries, each with its own membership requirements) is a professional organization of individual trainers who state that they are committed to becoming better trainers through education. The APDT features three levels of membership: professional, associate, and subscription. In some cases, membership is a personal decision about how active one wants to be in the organization since subscription members do not have voting privileges, yet they may be quite active as trainers. A list of member trainers is available on APDT's website to help individuals locate one in their area and what to look for in a training class.

APDT also has rally obedience (Rally-O) to encourage participation in the sport with an emphasis on having fun. Mixed breeds are welcome. A description of the sport is on the website and APDT has a Rally-O discussion list.

For information: apdt.com.

NATIONAL ASSOCIATION OF DOG OBEDIENCE INSTRUCTORS, INC. (NADOI)

NADOI was founded in 1965 to elevate the standards of the dog training profession, to mutually help both the dog and the human, and to designate certain members as having attained certain skills and knowledge. Their website has resources, their mission statement, events, and a list of instructors by state. The NADOI membership procedure is designed to evaluate an instructor's abilities, but they can be using virtually any training methodologies, although they do say that their instructors provide competent training using humane methods of teaching. NADOI is the oldest organization of its kind in the world and is international in scope.

For information: nadoi.org; e-mail available via the website; NADOI, PMB 369, 729 Grapevine Hwy., Hurst, TX 76054-2085.

INTERNATIONAL

ASSOCIATION OF PET DOG TRAINERS AUSTRALIA, INC.

The APDT in Australia is another association committed to the education of trainers with a goal of providing cutting-edge information and a forum for discussion and exchange of dog-training ideas. Their mission statement is, "To enhance the human-dog relationship by educating trainers, other animal professionals, and the public and advocating dog-friendly training." Their vision statement is, "All dogs are effectively trained through dog-friendly techniques and therefore are lifelong companions in a relationship based on mutual trust and respect."

Their trainers have a code of ethics which is available to the public on their website.

For information: apdt.com.au.

ASSOCIATION OF PET DOG TRAINERS (APDT) (UNITED KINGDOM)

"Kind-fair-effective" is the motto of APDT in the United Kingdom. Founded in 1995 by noted trainer John Fisher, they offer puppy and dog owners a guarantee of quality when looking for puppy or dog training classes in their area. This organization's members are trainers who provide positive instruction. Membership is restricted to professional dog trainers, unlike some other organizations that will allow anyone with an interest in training to join. The website is quite helpful for the pet dog owner. Not only can you find your nearest APDT member, but the website also has articles on finding the right puppy and what to look for when deciding on a training class. The site also has helpful advice on common training problems. It is also features a section allowing you to view and book courses if you want to further your education about dog training and behavior.

A subscriber list is available for £15 (to cover postage and printing costs) so nonmembers who want to further their dog-training knowledge can receive news and information about APDT members' activities, events, articles, and offers. Subscribers receive the three APDT newsletters a year, a county printout of members in their area, details of how to join the library, an invitation to join the APDT forum, and priority on organized events.

For information: apdt.co.uk.

CANADIAN ASSOCIATION OF PROFESSIONAL PET DOG TRAINERS (CAPPDT)

The CAPPDT's website proclaims that they are trainers sharing resources and education for the betterment of dogs and dog training in Canada. Their first priority as trainers is to the welfare of the dogs. The members actively promote ethical training, breeding, selling, and care of dogs. They are committed to humane training practices.

The website features training articles for the pet dog owner on such topics as separation anxiety, dogs and babies, and critical puppy periods. Their code of ethics is also available on the website.

For information: cappdt.ca.

POSITIVE TRAINING

The best training uses positive methods of teaching dogs, building a bond of trust between dog and owner, and making learning a fun experience. The dog trainer shows the owner how to teach the dog the basic skills he must have to be a good companion and welcomed guest wherever he goes.

A popular method of positive training is clicker training. The clicker is an event marker telling your dog that he has done what you want. You click when you see what you want (like a sit) to capture it and then give the dog an immediate reward. The system works because it teaches what you want and doesn't rely on punishing what you don't want. The dog soon learns that doing what you want earns him a reward.

BEST BEHAVIOR DOG TRAINING

Morgan Spector is one of the most respected clicker trainers in the world. His book, *Clicker Training for Obedience*, is pretty much the bible on the subject. Spector teaches operant conditioning (clicker training) for competition obedience, agility, service, and assistance dogs. He conducts private training and small-group classes of six and fewer. Spector has recently formed a partnership with Fran Jewell, Puppy Dog Training LLC, in Hailey, Idaho, where he can be expected to give seminars. The Best Behavior website links to the Puppy Dog Training LLC website. Information about upcoming events as well as classes in Idaho can be found online.

For information: bestbehavior.net; e-mail: morgan@bestbehavior.net.

CANINE SPORTS CENTER AT DIAMOND CREEK

Canine Sports Center at Diamond Creek is on a sixty-three-acre property in Goshen, Connecticut. This family-owned center offers classes and seminars in a variety of activities you and your dog might like to try, from conformation handling classes to pet obedience, competition obedience, rally obedience, and agility. All training classes use positive reinforcement.

At Canine Sports Center, they state that owning a dog is a privilege; a member of a different species is living with you, and his or her needs are your responsibility. Responsible pet ownership includes training as well as the answers to the basic questions of dog ownership. Canine Sports Center incorporates understanding canine behavior into their obedience classes. They also have grooming available as well as boarding at Diamond Creek Kennels that features air conditioning, radiant heat, and music. They also have a supply shop and a variety of events. The facility can also be rented.

For information: caninesportscenter.com; telephone: 860-491-3904; fax: 860-491-3906; Canine Sports Center at Diamond Creek, 416 Old Middle St., Rte. 63, Goshen, CT 06756. (Office hours are Monday through Friday, 8 A.M. to 1 P.M. and 4:30 P.M. to 6:30 P.M.; Saturday, 8 A.M. to 12 noon; and Sunday, 8 A.M. to 11 A.M., EST.)

CLICKER LOGIC

Clicker Logic is the website belonging to Texan Kellie Snider, who is in the Dallas–Fort Worth area. She teaches individuals and does behavior counseling. Having studied for a degree in behavior analysis combined with experience with clicker training, she is a positive trainer. Her website provides many resources for dog owners and she organizes seminars for dog owners, bringing notable guest speakers to the area. Information about forthcoming seminars can be found on the website. She also has training items for sale through her website, including clickers. You can also join the Clicker Logic information-only mailing list.

For information: clickerlogic.com; e-mail: kellie@clickerlogic.com; telephone: 972-650-8456.

CLICKERTRAINING.COM

Not a trainer, per se, but Karen Pryor's website is devoted to clicker training (operant conditioning). Pryor is responsible for popularizing this positive, easy way to train dogs. She had been the head trainer at Sea Life Park in Hawaii and when training other animals, she has applied the principles of the operant conditioning that she used when she worked with dolphins. Her website is largely devoted to training dogs as well as to cats and horses.

Pryor's publishing company, Sunshine Books, has published training books for various species including dogs. The books, as well as training equipment, are available at her website. You will also find a list of clicker training seminars, articles, and shelter resources. She even features a section for training humans. You can also sign up for a free newsletter.

For information: clickertraining.com.

HAPPY GO LUCKY DOG TRAINING AND PLAYCARE

Happy Go Lucky's mission at is to "improve the quality of life for dogs and their people" and they were Portland's first day care for dogs. They have positive obedience classes based on knowledge, communication, trust, and fun, including puppy kindergarten and intermediate- and advanced-level classes. They also offer private instruction. Their "play-care" is supervised by a trainer in two buildings totaling more than 4,500 square feet. Before enrolling your dog in playcare, he will be evaluated by appointment to be sure everyone will have fun. Your dog must be dog and people friendly, five months of age or older, healthy and current on all vaccinations, spayed or neutered after six months of age, and on an effective flea prevention program. A typical day features playtime, snack time, and naptime. Other classes at Happy Go Lucky include Out-on-the-Town, Intro to Agility, Canine Good Citizen, and Tricks and Games.

The starting age for puppy kindergarten is ten to sixteen weeks (small breeds up to twenty weeks). The class meets for six weeks. The first class is 1½ hours, without your dog. Beginning obedience can be started when your dog is four months old. The first class is also 1½ hours without your dog, and the course runs for six weeks. Details of all classes can be found on the website, including the two intermediate levels and the advanced levels.

The Out-on-the-Town class meets at different, preselected locations each week, such as parks, the waterfront, or restaurants, working on skills such as loose-leash walking, come, and leave it with distractions. Happily, no choke collars or pinch collars are used during training. They offer discounts if you have two dogs entered in classes, and there's a shelter/rescue dog discount as well, which only applies to beginning obedience or puppy kindergarten classes. A schedule of classes is on the website, or you can contact them for more information.

For information: happygoluckydog.com; e-mail: info@happygolucky dog.com; telephone: 503-731-8774; Happy Go Lucky, 1642 N.E. Sandy Blvd., Portland, OR. (Playcare hours: drop-off is at 7:15 A.M. or later; pickup is at 6:00 P.M. A late pickup fee applies after 6:10 P.M. Reservation cancellations must be made by noon the prior day.)

LEGACY

Sequim, Washington, is the home of Legacy, headed by Terry Ryan. Along with dog-training classes from puppy to adult, she runs a camp each summer, bringing in such notables as Morgan Spector, Kathy Sdao, and Bob Bailey. She also has courses for instructors and her website is also available in Japanese. Why Japanese? Terry Ryan goes to Japan each year to teach, taking other instructors with her. She presents a variety of programs in Japan for the Japanese Animal Hospital Association, the Animal Fanciers' Club, and the Japan Good Citizen's Group. Additionally, there are motivational classes year-round in Japan. In the United States, Terry Ryan also gives private lessons; of course she has other qualified instructors at Legacy.

For information: legacycanine.com; e-mail: info@legacycanine.com; telephone: 360-683-1522; fax: 360-683-1568; Legacy, P.O. Box 3909, Sequim, WA 98382.

MASTERPEACE DOG TRAINING

This training center defines itself as "Peaceful training for dog and master." They state that they use "time proven positive training methods." They teach owners to communicate with their dog without stress or anger and they keep training sessions fun. Their classes range from puppy kindergarten and beginning pet classes through competitive obedience, for those who choose to participate in obedience as a sport. They teach owners not just the basics, but the principles behind the training so that they will continue throughout the dog's lifetime. They also leave time for questions and answers in each class, so individual issues can be addressed. MasterPeace also has agility classes, flyball, and breed-handling classes as well. And they have canine good citizen sessions and tests. MasterPeace also offers doggie day care which runs from 7 A.M. to 6 P.M. with a choice of full or half day sessions. Half days are available from a choice of 7 A.M. to 12 noon, or 1 P.M. to 6 P.M. Day care allows your dog to play with others, instead of being alone all day while you're at work. Your dog will be tired and relaxed when you pick him up. They offer two-hour playgroups by appointment, a nice way to see if your dog gets along well with others before you leave him for an entire day of day care. They also have Friday night playgroups. MasterPeace hosts a variety of events for dogs and owners and a special section on their website is devoted to these listings.

For information: masterpeacedog.com; e-mail: info@masterpeacedog.com; telephone: 508-553-9300; MasterPeace Dog Training, 264 Fisher St., Franklin, MA 02038.

NEW YORK DOG SPA & HOTEL

New York City is the home to the New York Dog Spa & Hotel for dogs. They have boarding, day care, grooming, training, and veterinary services. The Dog Spa was designed by architect William Bowick. It has a state-of-the-art ventilation–air-conditioning system using 100 percent fresh air to eliminate odors and protect from airborne organisms.

Most of the dogs boarded spend the day in the day-care facility, where they interact with other dogs of similar size and temperament and are under the watchful eye of trained attendants. Each dog gets a private run or cage, depending upon size, for sleeping and eating. Dogs that are being boarded are walked twice a day for a break in their routine and to get fresh air and take care of business. Additional walks can be arranged at a nominal charge. You can bring toys, pet beds, or blankets, but they ask that you bring nothing of real value because things can be chewed. Dogs may arrive from 7 A.M. to 8 P.M. and may be picked up from 8 A.M. to 10 P.M., seven days per week. Reservations are required but they can often accommodate last-minute reservations.

They offer on-site veterinary service, supervised by the director of Lexington Veterinary Group PC. Dogs requiring more advanced treatment will be transported to the veterinary hospital by New York Dog

Spa at no charge. Veterinary service office hours are by appointment only. Grooming, bathing, and doggie massage are available by appointment. Dog training is available offering the Sirius Puppy Training Program developed by Dr. Ian Dunbar. They have an online boutique where owners can purchase a variety of items including coats and sweaters, designer bowls, and other items.

For information: dogspa.com; e-mail: nydogspa@aol.com; telephone (both locations): 212-243-1199; fax: 212-414-0422; New York Dog Spa, 145 West 18th St., New York, NY 10011; and 32 West 25th St., New York, NY 10010.

PAWS AND PETS

The owner of Paws and Pets, in Florida's Sarasota area, has experience in animal training and care since 1968. A personal dog trainer, professional poodle groomer, professional horse trainer and instructor, service dog trainer, and wildlife rehabilitator, Linda Carter, P.D.T., is a member of APDT as well as the American Association of Assistance Dog Partners and the North American Flyball Association, and she is an AKC Canine Good Citizen Evaluator as well as an Assistance/Service Dog Public Access Certification Test Evaluator.

Only positive training methods are used with positive training focusing on ignoring what you want to extinguish and rewarding what you want repeated. No choke chains, prong collars, or excessive force is used. She gives private lessons or group sessions in your home. There is an additional charge if she must travel more than ten miles. She focuses on clicker training, which is fun and easy. You can find a good description of clicker training and a sample exercise to try at the website.

For information: pawsandpets.com; e-mail: linda@pawsandpets.com; telephone: 941-927-2757.

THE PAWSITIVE DOG, INC.

The Pawsitive Dog, Inc., "a heart to paw connection bringing harmony to life . . . one relationship at a time," is based in Illinois. The

Pawsitive Dog's goal is to improve communication between dogs and humans, and their love for dogs is apparent in the way they train. They provide in-person, one-to-one training and only positive training methods are used. They use their years of experience, as well as their knowledge of classical and operant conditioning, to help owners resolve behavior issues in the most nonstressful way. At The Pawsitive Dog, Inc., you'll find force-free training that the entire family can do. They also sell a "dog in training" vest. This is not the attire of a service dog, but is something to use to identify your dog as still in training so the general public will understand that your dog is a work in progress and that you're working with him or her. This is especially helpful when the dog has a behavior problem that needs work and can help the owner get over their fear of embarrassment, allowing the owner to relax and focus on the dog. When the owner and the public are more relaxed, true learning and change can begin to occur. Ordering information is on their website.

For information: pawsitivedog.com; e-mail: info@pawsitivedog.com; telephone: 309-699-6935; The Pawsitive Dog, P.O. Box 185, Groveland, IL 61535.

POSITIVE PET PEOPLE

Positive Pet People is located in Athens, Georgia. Their positive training methods are designed to help strengthen the bond between dogs and their owners. They have classes, private consultations, training workshops, and headcollar training packages. However, they primarily use a clicker (operant conditioning) in their training. They welcome visitors who call ahead. Among the classes they offer are puppy preschool, a starter class, an advanced class, and a class for competitive obedience. They have a "Rowdy Rovers" class for dogs who bark, lunge, or growl at other dogs while on leash; the class teaches them to relax and have better manners around other dogs. Enthusiasm, patience, and good humor are among the things they recommend that you bring to class. Classes are held at The Athens Animal Health Center. The trainers are a woman with a Ph.D. in psychology who is currently training to become a veterinarian, and a dog trainer with a master's degree who competes in tracking and obedience. They also carry a variety of training products that are also available at their website.

For information: positivepetpeople.com; e-mail: info@positivepet people.com; telephone and fax: 706-548-2508; Positive Pet People, P.O. Box 81294, Athens, GA 30608.

PUPPY PLAYLAND

Puppy Playland's slogan and philosophy is, "helping dogs find their inner puppy." They are a full-service doggie day care that also offers grooming, training, education, event planning, and a shop called Chez Paw. Puppy Playland has an experienced staff who can answer questions on a broad range of topics. Their memberships include APDT, the American Boarding Kennel Association, and the Better Business Bureau.

Day care is available to all dogs three months of age and older, but they must have completed their initial puppy vaccinations, which include DHPP and Bordatella. They must have proof of current vaccines including rabies yearly and must have been in good health for thirty days prior to attending day care. All dogs must go in for an "interview" so they can be assessed regarding how they will respond to a group situation. Dogs are interviewed on an individual basis, including mixed breeds and rescue dogs. The dog must have lived with you for six months prior to attending day care unless the dog is less than six months old. A new home can be a stressful situation for a dog, and Puppy Playland wants the dog to be comfortable in their new home so the day-care environment won't stress him.

All dogs older than eight months must be spayed or neutered. Older or out of shape dogs must have a note from their veterinarian saying that they can participate in moderate exercise without health risk. Puppy Playland maintains a ratio of one person for every ten to fifteen dogs so that they can be sure that each dog receives enough attention.

Each dog receives exercise, play, and socialization. In addition to group play, each dog receives individual attention throughout the day.

Each day is different. Rest periods throughout the day ensure that the dogs don't become overtired. They also use agility equipment designed to build confidence in dogs. Rubber matting is found in the entire play area for better traction and to reduce stress injuries. And they have a quiet room for dogs who want to spend some time on the couch.

You can log onto the website and watch your dog via their puppy-cam. They use hospital-grade disinfectant for cleaning and have an air-purification system. They are open Monday through Friday, 7 A.M. to 7 P.M. They have discount programs for advance reservations, rescue dogs, and multiple-dog families, as well as multivisit discounts. Full-service grooming is available Tuesday through Saturday mornings, by appointment.

Puppy Playland also has a wide variety of training classes from beginning as well as level two obedience classes. They offer agility classes, conformation, confidence-building classes, and a "Dogs Can Dance" class. Check for flyball and rally obedience as well. Education classes are available for owners that include seminars on Tellington TTouch, therapy dogs, and animal communication.

They have been the site for the Southwest Regional Competition of the World Canine Freestyle Organization. Many clubs and organizations hold events at Puppy Playland where you can also hold a birthday party for your dog if you're so inclined.

For information: puppyplayland.com; e-mail: info@puppyplayland .com; telephone: 925-725-2300 (Phone hours are during regular business hours, Monday through Friday, 7 A.M. to 7 P.M.; voice mail is available after hours.); fax: 925-725-2301; Puppy Playland, 2556 San Ramon Valley Blvd., San Ramon, CA.

SAN FRANCISCO SOCIETY FOR THE PREVENTION OF CRUELTY TO ANIMALS (SFSPCA)

The SFSPCA is a private, nonprofit welfare organization, dedicated to saving and providing medical care to needy and/or homeless dogs and cats. They find loving homes for strays and are proactive regarding humane education. The SFSPCA holds training and behavior classes, all under the guidance of Jean Donaldson, author of a number of books, including *Mine*. Their behavior and training department offers extensive programs of classes for the public from puppy classes and basic obedience to courses in clicker training, agility, and flyball. The behavior program helps owners better understand their dogs. They also offer periodic behavior seminars.

They do have a few requirements for classes, including: proof of rabies vaccination and for Puppy Basic, proof of two rounds of DHLPP vaccinations, a flat collar (no choke, prong, or shock collars) or a Gentle Leader, a five- to six-foot lead (no retractable leashes), poop bags for cleanup, and a hungry dog and a variety of your dog's favorite treats cut into small pieces. All classes meet in the multipurpose room of the SFSPCA.

The SFSPCA also rehabilitates shelter dogs with behavior problems to ensure that they can be placed in loving homes. They have an academy for dog trainers, led by Donaldson. The SFSPCA also has a free, troubleshooting animal-behavior hotline.

The SFSPCA website contains useful information, including an online library of articles. To find out more about them check at the website or give them a call at the number that follows. They also offer cat behavior classes.

For information: sfspca.org; e-mail: dogtraining@sfspca.org; telephone (main): 415-554-3000 or (to register for classes or get more information): 415-522-3509 or 415-522-3565; fax: 415-522-7041; The San Francisco SPCA, 2500 16th St., San Francisco, CA 94103-4213.

STACY'S WAG'N'TRAIN

Located in the San Jose, California, area, Stacy's Wag'N'Train promises to teach owners how to communicate their rules to their dog while enhancing the relationship between owner and four-legged family member. By using clicker training, the owner learns how a dog learns. They do not just teach the obedience exercises used in competition rings. Instead, they concentrate on teaching skills such as greeting people nicely at the door; loose-leash walking; and calmly accepting the touch of their veterinarian, groomer, or a child. This prevents behavior problems before they start. Unlike correction-based, aversive training, clicker training can be started when the puppy is fairly young—it's like a wonderful game that he's learning to play. Training at Stacy's Wag'N'Train can begin as soon as the puppy has had his first shots. Training classes include Puppy Kindergarten, Companion Dog I, Companion Dog II, Fun Tricks, and Intro to Agility for Fun. They also offer behavior modification for those who need it. A weekly Toydog social gathering is offered specifically for small dogs, allowing them to feel comfortable with other dogs who are their own size, not bigger and heavier. They can enjoy safer play without risk of accidental injury.

The website gives more information about clicker training, including the wide range of dogs who benefit from its use. A links page lists dog and training events in San Jose and the Bay Area. And, you can find tips.

In an effort to support responsible dog ownership and adopting shelter or rescue group dogs, a 10 percent discount is offered for all spayed or neutered dogs. Private lessons in your home are available. Classes are held at two, well-lit, indoor and heated locations: at Bird and Montgomery, near downtown San Jose, and where Capital Expressway crosses Highway 101.

For information: wagntrain.com; e-mail: stacy@wagntrain.com; telephone: 408-286-3889. **Class locations:** Downtown Dogs, 564 W. San Carlos St., San Jose, CA and Pet Food Express, 1787 E. Capital Expressway, San Jose, CA 95121.

TAILS-A-WAGGING DOGGIE DAYCARE

Tails-A-Wagging is a day-care facility with more to offer. Day care is an option when you work or have a full day of errands and your dog would otherwise be left on his own. For the dog who doesn't share his life with another dog, this is an opportunity to interact with others in a supervised environment.

At Tails-A-Wagging, each potential day-care member receives a private temperament screening prior to acceptance. Dogs who are aggressive are not accepted. All dogs must be up to date on vaccinations and adult dogs must be spayed or neutered and free from internal and external parasites. No breed is automatically eliminated; however, certain health problems will preclude admittance such as blindness and seizure-type disorders. Each newcomer is individually introduced to the other dogs, which can take from six to eight hours and is done under the watchful, trained eye of a staff member.

Those contemplating day care are welcome to visit at anytime. They are open Monday through Friday, 7 A.M. to 6 P.M. Early morning and late afternoon, however, are very busy because of dogs being dropped off and picked up.

The facility has more than four-hundred square feet of indoor and outdoor play areas. They have soft futons for dogs to sleep on, epoxy floors inside for cushion, lots of durable toys suited for tough play, and access to water at all times. They also have live Webcams on their website, so you can watch the dogs. The outdoor yard is fully fenced and the area is cleaned and sanitized. They have several areas at day care where small dogs can play together and separate rooms so the little dogs can be separated for different games.

The day is structured much as it would be for human day care, with nap time and playtimes. Dogs are always taken aside and fed alone. The co-owners are both certified in pet CPR and first aid. They have a BarkMobile Pet Transport if you need your pet picked up or taken home, but arrangements for transportation must be made in advance. For dogs who won't fit well into day care, they have professional pet-sitting services. A sitter can go to your home during the day or while you're away on vacation or business. They do more than just take care of pets. A full description of services is available at their website. They are licensed, bonded, and insured.

Dog training is also available with classes structured for various levels from basic beginner, in which the owner also learns theory and training methods, to advanced. They also have a trick training class, which is fun for both dog and owner. Private lessons are also available. All teaching methods are based on positive reinforcement. Verbal praise, food, toys, and clicker training are some of their motivators. They want to make training safe and fun for dogs and owners. Their website also has an events page.

For information: tails-a-wagging.com; e-mail: info@tails-a-wagging
.com; telephone: 360-733-PETS; Tails-A-Wagging, 2123 Lincoln St.,
Bellingham, WA.

TAILS-U-WIN CANINE CENTER, LLC

Tails-U-Win in Manchester, Connecticut, is owned by trainer and lecturer Leslie Nelson, who is well known for her Really Reliable Recall.
They opened in 1991 and, at last count, had eighteen instructors con-
ducting forty-five classes a week. Many of the instructors are nationally recognized with many areas of expertise.

Training methods for all classes at this facility are purely positive.
Classes are family-oriented, fun, and effective. They meet weekly and
are offered days, nights, and weekends. Classes are kept small, so preregistration is required and fees are not refundable after classes have
started. Dogs need proof of current rabies vaccination. They offer family dog classes at various levels, puppy kindergarten, and companion
and therapy training for graduates of family dog II. You can also sign
your dog up for a versatility class if he has completed family dog I, II,
or puppy kindergarten if you want to do something more with your
dogs but haven't yet chosen an activity. This class offers a taste of many
including disc, agility, freestyle, tracking, flyball, competition obedience, massage, and therapy dog work.

They also offer TTouch classes, as well as classes in competition
obedience, agility, breed handling, flyball, freestyle, rally obedience,
leash walking, clicker tricks, and more. Along with classes, Tails-U-
Win offers private instruction as well as behavior consultations. You are
welcome to visit at any time. The building and grounds are used for
all sorts of canine activities. They host seminars and put on training
matches throughout the year. They also rent the building to clubs for
their events and shows. And, they donate space to a therapy dog group,
sponsor a flyball team, and a local positively powered police canine
unit trains there after hours. During the day, part of the space is sub-
let to a doggie day care. Tails-U-Win also provides memberships and
has more than one hundred active members who use the facility to

train privately or with friends. A second center, Tails-U-Win, Too! has been opened in Simsbury, Connecticut.

For information: tailsuwin.com; e-mail: info@tailsuwin.com; telephone: 860-646-5033 or (Tails-U-Win, Too!): 860-370-9623; Tails-U-Win Canine Center, LLC, 175 Adams St., Manchester, CT 06040.

INTERNATIONAL

CAROLARK—CENTRE FOR APPLIED CANINE BEHAVIOUR

Those in the province of Ontario, Canada, can find positive training at Carolark, the Centre for Applied Canine Behavior owned by Carolyn Clark. Her mission statement reads, "Our mission is to provide the best training possible for people and their dogs, emphasizing a positive people/pet relationship in an atmosphere of care, friendliness, professionalism, and respect for our clients, their dogs, and ourselves. All of the staff of the training centre is committed to helping owners enjoy that special relationship, or bond, that can exist between owner and dog."

Carolark not only offers regular training classes for puppies through adults, but specific ones such as loose-leash walking and a reactive dog class. They also host special guest instructors who present workshops, such as chicken training, which sharpens one's clicker training skills, and calming signals with Turid Rugaas of Norway. Carolark also has Rally-O classes, which are becoming increasingly popular.

For information: carolark.com; e-mail: carolark@igs.net; telephone (toll-free): 877-763-6664 or (local): 613-591-3277; fax: 613-591-0419; Centre for Applied Canine Behavior, 600 Eagleson Rd., Kanata, ON K2M 1H4, Canada. (Office hours are Monday through Thursday, 8:30 A.M. to 3:30 P.M.)

DOGSMART

DogSmart is a professional dog-training and behavior-consulting company in Vancouver, British Columbia. They do private consultations as well as group dog-training classes and offer programs in Vancouver, Burnaby, North Delta, and private consultations throughout the Lower Mainland. Their training methods are positive and are designed to strengthen the bond between dog and owner. They state that the programs are nonabusive and motivational. You will have to complete their beginner's course before going on to either more advanced courses or the fun-and-games or out-and-about classes. Out-and-about classes are held in a variety of places so the dog learns to use his skills in real-life situations. Puppies can start their puppy socialization and training classes as early as ten weeks of age. Any dog in need of training at any age will start as a beginner. The training includes life skills, along with the usual basic obedience. Off-leash training is usually started in the intermediate class. They also teach clicker training classes and a five-week canine good citizen course, which prepares the dog to pass the Canadian Canine Good Citizen test, given during the fifth class. And they have agility classes at a variety of levels. DogSmart will help place the individual and their dog in the right programs. They also hold a variety of events, including an agility fun match, and puppy socialization. They also sell a variety of positive-training books and videos.

For information: dogsmart.bc.ca; e-mail: dogsmart@telus.net; telephone: Delores Wall, CPDT at 604-267-9500; DogSmart, 8206 Ontario St., Vancouver, BC V5X 3E3, Canada.

DREAM FIELDS DOG AGILITY TRAINING CENTRE

Dream Fields, located in Ottawa, Ontario, specializes in agility training, from puppy through advanced. The sport of dog agility involves the dog running an obstacle course, with the owner running along and giving him cues. The dog with the fastest time without errors wins the highest score. It's fun for both dog and owner. The agility course involves everything from a slalom of weave poles to a tunnel, jumping through a tire, and on and on it goes. It's both fun and challenging and allows the dog to gain confidence as well as run off excess energy. All breeds, including mixed breeds, can run an agility course. Jumps are set to accommodate the dog's size so even toy dogs can participate.

Dream Fields uses only motivational training. And no dog is asked to do something it is not ready to do.

For information: dreamfields.com; e-mail: dreamfld@istar.ca; telephone: 613-832-5898; Dream Fields, P.O. Box 144, Dunrobin, ON K0A 1T0, Canada.

WAGGIN' TAILS K9 PLAYSCHOOL

Waggin' Tails K9 Playschool is a doggie day care facility in Canada. Their goal is your dog's safety and happiness in a stress-free environment. They specialize in a unique personalized service with each dog receiving special care and attention.

They have limited space and request that owners book at least twenty-four hours in advance. And, they ask that you give your dog an opportunity to relieve himself before entering Waggin' Tails. New dogs are screened daily, and all dogs must enter and leave the building on leash. Waggin' Tails works with timid or fearful dogs, so it's important that everyone entering and leaving the building remain calm and quiet.

All dogs must have a buckle collar; leash; and Halti or Gentle Leader, if you use a halter system, for your dog to be walked during the day. You'll have to bring along your dog's food if he requires a meal during his stay, as well as specific instructions, or any supplements. A dish will be provided.

Your dog should not have too much stimulation before arriving at day care since he will have ample opportunity to work off that excess energy at Waggin' Tails. They also have training classes, introductory agility, and rally obedience, all done with positive training.

They offer grooming by appointment. Each dog is walked and played with before being groomed and the grooming facility is cageless. Waggin' Tails has five thousand square feet of space with indoor and outdoor play areas. Daily park walks are included with dogs going to the park in pairs. The dog lounge includes TV couch and toys.

Prices are available on the website, and they offer packages and a taxi service for an additional fee. They have expanded to an overnight service where the dogs are never kenneled and never left alone. And they also offer in-house individual dog walking—no groups!

For information: waggintails.ca; e-mail: dogs@waggintails.ca; telephone: 604-990-TAIL; Waggin' Tails, 1340 Pemberton Ave., North Vancouver, BC V7P 2R7, Canada. (Hours are Monday through Saturday, 7 A.M. to 7 P.M., and Sunday by appointment at a higher rate. Holidays are available at double the usual rate.)

HAPPY PETS

Dr. Attila Szkukalek is in charge of Happy Pets in England. He specializes in behavior therapy and training and does one-to-one dog and cat training for pets with problem behaviors. He also conducts regular classes for pets and their owners. He and his instructors teach a puppy socialization class appropriately called The Little Rascals that is geared to puppies between two to four months old, as soon as their vaccinations are complete. Positive training methods are used and the course includes the theory of socialization and environment habituation as well as how animals learn. Advice is given about frequent puppy behavior concerns like mouthing, jumping up, and house-training, as well as bite inhibition. The course teaches puppies to enjoy being handled, to have basic manners, and to come when called, sit, lie down, and stay. Other courses include good manners obedience training, and fun classes for dogs to improve their responsiveness. Classes take place at the "Marlpit" Community Center in Norwich.

Szkukalek also offers dog-rhythmics, or canine musical freestyle. He is one the world's best freestylers and has created two training videos that are among the very finest. They can be purchased from Happy Pets in the United Kingdom and are available in the United States through the World Canine Freestyle Organization, Inc.

For information: all-dogs-cats.cwc.net; e-mail: attila@happypets.fsnet .co.uk; telephone: 01603611184; Dr. Attila Szkukalek, 84 Strafford St., Norwich NR2 38G, United Kingdom.

SHEILA HARPER

Best known in England, along with several others who have worked with her (collectively as Scallywags), Sheila Harper is a full-time teacher interested in problem behavior. She is an associate of the UK

Registry of Canine Behaviorists and also a member of APDT (U.K.) and Pet Dog Trainers of Europe. Scallywags Education Center was begun in 1993 to help dogs and owners learn to have fun together. Harper's international dog-trainers school features guest lecturers, and she runs summer camps for you and your dogs. From professional pet trainers to pet owners, she provides a wealth of information and only the gentlest teaching methods. To keep with her philosophy that promotes kindness, and teaches understanding of canine behavior, training, and gentle handling, calming signals and the work of Turid Rugaas are among the positive and progressive issues discussed. Harper's prime concern is to promote a respectful and harmonious relationship between dog and owner and to encourage owners to increase their knowledge and experience.

For information: scallywagsf9.co.uk; e-mail: sheila@scallywags.force9 .co.uk; telephone: 01889 802685; Sheila Harper, 9 The Meadows, Rugeley, Staffs WS15 1JH, United Kingdom.

TURID RUGAAS—HAGAN HUNDESKOLE

Yes, Turid Rugaas of Norway is the noted, groundbreaking trainer and lecturer whose book, videos, and seminars are changing the way people around the world look at dogs. She is also president of Pet Dog Trainers of Europe. You don't have to live in Norway to take advantage of her expertise. She travels extensively, lecturing around the world. It is well worth your while to not only surf her website for information, but to check her lecture schedule and take advantage of a seminar in your own country. Hagan Hundeskole translates quite simply as: dog school. And Rugaas's website appears in English as well as Norwegian. She offers this simple, but profound statement of her lofty goal: "to educate dog trainers that are able to help dogs and owners to a better life together." She wants to "promote ethical opinions in dog care, better understanding of the dogs' behavior, and why problems are arising."

Rugaas's courses for dog trainers are held in Germany and last approximately one year and are built on the natural behavior of dogs. She teaches how to solve problems, creative training instruction technique, consultation technique, and more. She accepts a maximum of eighteen students. More information is available on the website. Rugaas also has camps in Norway with stress-free agility, flyball, tracking, freestyle, and more fun activities once or twice a year, along with week-end courses.

For information: turid-rugaas.no/ukfront.htm; e-mail: turidrug@ frisurf.no; telephone: 47 32 78 09 87; Hagan Hundeskole, Turid Rugaas, Postboks 109, 3361 Geithus, Norway.

CANINE GOOD CITIZEN TESTS

Canine good citizen programs are available in several countries including the United States, Canada, and the United Kingdom. The tests are designed to show that a dog can deal with everyday life occurrences. In the United States, the AKC's Canine Good Citizen test can be taken by any dog, purebred or mixed breed. The dog must pass a series of tests, including waiting while the owner is out of sight, not reacting when something like an umbrella is opened, and sitting politely for petting. Some cities and towns will give the owner a discount on the dog's registration fee if it can be shown that the dog has passed the Canine Good Citizen test.

In England, The Kennel Club Good Citizen Dog educates owners and their dogs and is now the largest national dog-training program in the United Kingdom. It developed from one initial award to four levels of dog-training education. This program is for mixed breed dogs as well as purebreds. In the United Kingdom, it was created to combat the growing antidog sentiments.

It's really a good idea for every dog to become a canine good citizen. Being able to pass these tests will also ensure that your dog is an ambassador for canines whenever and wherever you travel.

FUN ACTIVITIES

Getting involved in a canine activity is one of the best gifts you can give to your dog and yourself. These activities can be fun, can strengthen the dog-owner bond, and participating in them is a great way to meet new friends.

DOG SCOUTS OF AMERICA

Scouting for dogs? You bet! And it's more than a camp. Dog Scouts of America is a nonprofit organization, founded in 1995 to encourage people to be more responsible dog owners and to promote the human-animal bond. Their motto is, "Let us learn new things, that we may become more helpful." Just like other scouting organizations, the participants earn merit badges, depicting the individual activities, for their skills in various activities. The badges can be displayed on the dog's backpack, Dog Scout Cape, crate cover, or travel bag. When the dogs aren't at camp, the owners are encouraged to pursue some of the activities they've learned or to get involved in community-service activities. Dog Scouts of America members are also invited on the weekend outings that occur periodically during the year.

For information: dogscouts.com; telephone: 989-389-2000; fax: 989-389-2267; Dog Scouts of America, 5068 Nestel Rd., St. Helen, MI 48656.

DOG ACTIVITIES

Here are some activities you can do with your dog that are fun and not only help to strengthen the bond between you and your dog, but will lead you to make friends who share your interest in both dogs and dog sports. Groups exist virtually all over the world. These are only a few of the available activities that you and your dog can try together. Some dogs and people are more suited to some sports than others. You and your dog will have fun finding your niche. Some activities, such as lure coursing; earthdog; water activities; herding; weight pull; snow activities, like mushing and skijoring; and carting are geared to specific breeds for whom the activity is what they were originally bred to do.

AGILITY

Agility gets the spectator's heart racing as much as the dog-owner team. The dog who competes in agility races against the clock while meeting the challenges of an obstacle course. The obstacles include a tunnel, ramps, weave poles, and jumps (with height set in relationship to the dog's height at the shoulder). You can compete locally just for fun or move up to more competitive levels. The AKC has a national competition and a world agility team. UKC also has agility competitions, as does the United States Dog Agility Association (USDAA), which markets agility as a spectator sport in its own right and promotes the standards as developed in the United Kingdom. USDAA is an affiliated member of the International Federation of Cynological Sport (IFCS) and sends a world team to the IFCS world championships held in Europe.

For information: usdaa.com; e-mail: info@usdaa.com; telephone: 972-487-2200; fax: 972-272-4404; United States Dog Agility Association (USDAA), P.O. Box 850955, Richardson, TX 75085-0955.

CANINE MUSICAL FREESTYLE

Canine musical freestyle is a choreographed dance routine with your dog that's set to music. The dance routines are a series of safe tricks and moves. This activity is sometimes called heelwork to music, but in the World Canine Freestyle Organization (WCFO)—the world's largest freestyle organization—these are two separate categories. Freestyle is catching on all over the world; anyone from children to seniors can participate, as can any dog, no matter his size or if he's purebred or of mixed heritage. This is a fun activity for everyone involved. In WCFO, the emphasis is on the bond between dog and human companion.

For information: worldcaninefreestyle.org; e-mail: wcfodogs@aol.com; telephone: 718-332-8336; fax: 718-646-2686; World Canine Freestyle Organization, P.O. Box 350122, Brooklyn, NY 11235-2525.

DISC DOG

Disc dog competitions take playing to another level. Dogs jump for flying discs. The toss-and-fetch aspects are judged in one category and another is called freestyle. Disc dog features a lot of jumping and fast turns. This is an active sport and your dog must be in good athletic condition.

Individual dog disc clubs mainly coordinate this sport. You can locate them via the USDDN website, which is maintained by Ron King. Click on the individual club's website and you will learn more about the club in your area as well as upcoming competitions.

For information: discdog.org; telephone: 317-281-3398; fax: 317-257-5918; United States Dog Disc National (USDDN) Championship Series, 635 N. DeQuincy St., Indianapolis, IN 46201.

FIELD EVENTS

Field trials and hunting tests are done by both AKC and UKC and take advantage of the instincts of individual breeds. They are open to Retrievers, pointing breeds, Spaniels, Beagles, Basset Hounds, and Dachshunds, and are geared to the breed's particular skills. It's a way to show that your dog can still do what he was originally bred to do and take advantage of your dog's natural instincts.

FLYBALL

Flyball is a relay race, in which teams of dogs race against the clock to run to a box, tap a pedal on it which releases a ball, catch the ball, and return to the starting point, thus sending the next dog down to the box until each in the team has run the race. The first team to finish wins. This is a fast-paced team sport.

For information: flyball.org; telephone and fax: 800-318-6312; North American Flyball Association (NAFA), 1400 W. Devon Ave., #512, Chicago, IL 60660.

OBEDIENCE

Obedience is a sport for those who want to take basic training into the ring and then progress to other levels. Your dog must perform a pre-scribed series of exercises. The dog is scored on the exercises. The two largest dog registries in the United States and the United Kingdom have obedience trials, although there are minor differences among them. The levels progress from the basics to the more advanced levels involving jumping and retrieving and scent discrimination. Each individual registry offers its own titles that your dog can earn. For those who participate in AKC sanctioned sports, they also offer a Versatile

Companion Dog award given to the dog who has been successful in multiple sports. Rally-O is a new form of obedience that's done for fun. Here, the dog and handler follow directions on signs around the course, rather than receive further instructions from the judge.

TRACKING

Tracking allows the dog to use his natural instinct for following human scent. This is an outdoor activity that provides plenty of exercise. Tracks are different, so the dog cannot anticipate one track being like the last one he followed. The more advanced he becomes, the "older" the track will be. In other words, the track is laid down more hours in advance of the competition. AKC and UKC offers their own competitions.

ORGANIZATIONS

The following is a list of organizations involved in dog sports. There are, of course, others, but these are the largest. Virtually every dog club around the world will be able to lead you to competitions in obedience, agility, and hunting and field events. Training classes are another good way to find competitions.

American Kennel Club (AKC): akc.org; e-mail: info@akc.org; telephone: 919-233-9767; fax: 919-816-3627; 5580 Centerview Dr., Raleigh, NC 27606-3390.

Australian Kennel Club: The Australian Kennel Club asks that for information about clubs or shows, individuals in Australia contact the State or Territory Controlling Body for their area. The contact information for each of these can be found at the website: ankc.aust.com.

Canadian Kennel Club: ckc.ca; telephone (toll-free): 800-250-8040, (local): 416-675-5511, or (client services): 416-674-3699; fax: 416-675-6506; 89 Skyway Ave., Suite 100, Etobicoke, ON M9W 6R4, Canada.

Irish Kennel Club: ikc.ie; telephone: (01) 4533300, 4532309, 4532310, or (outside Ireland): +353-1-4533300; fax: (01) 4533237 or (outside Ireland): +353-1-4533237; Fottrell House, Harold's Cross Bridge, Dublin 6W, Ireland.

The Kennel Club: the-kennel-club.org.uk; telephone: 0807 606 6750; fax: 020 7518 1058; 1-5 Clarges St., London W1J 8AB, United Kingdom.

New Zealand Kennel Club: nzkc.org.nz; telephone: (04) 237 4489; fax: (04) 237 0721; Prosser St., Private Bag 50903, Porirua 6220, New Zealand.

United Kennel Club: ukcdogs.com; telephone: 269-343-9020; fax: 269-343-7037; 100 E. Kilgore Rd., Kalamazoo, MI 49002-5584.

DOG PARKS

Some people love dog parks, others don't. It can be a way for your dog to meet and interact with other dogs and give him an opportunity to run off-leash. How good the experience is will depend on many things. If you decide to go to one, you should look for some things to make the experience the best one possible for you and your dog.

A dog park, in this sense, is a place where your dog is allowed to run and play with other dogs in a certain area. Not all parks allow dogs, but dog parks are special areas set up precisely for this activity. Some dog parks have fences, others don't. A dog park without a fence can be a hazard if your dog doesn't always come when you call him. Or, he could bolt out into traffic if he becomes startled or is so busy running he's not paying much attention to where he's going.

To ensure that the visit is as safe as possible, all puppies and dogs should be vaccinated and be free from contagious diseases as well as being free of both internal and external parasites. The dog park should be supervised by the owners who are present, and all dogs should be trained to respond to the basics: come, sit, down, stay, leave it. Everyone should have a dog-friendly dog, but that may not always be the case. Dogs that are aggressive toward other dogs or people, or who in any way show any threatening behavior, shouldn't be allowed to enter the dog park. This is for everyone's safety.

Before you enter the dog park, ask people who are there about any unfamiliar (to you) dogs who are present before you enter. And do spend some time watching the body language of the dogs who are already in the park. This can help to prevent dogfights. If you have a small dog, perhaps lighter than twenty pounds, be aware of possible dangers from very rowdy dogs, Sighthounds, or very large dogs who may view your little one as prey. Some big dogs are wonderful with little dogs, but others are not. Bitches in season shouldn't be in the dog park for obvious reasons.

Before entering, observe for awhile to make sure that owners are supervising their own dog(s) at all times and that if they must leave for a few minutes, they are taking their dog with them. The dog park should be clean, with owners cleaning up after their own dog. It's easy to bring some plastic bags for this purpose.

If the dog park is in a congested city area, owners should make all attempts to keep barking to a minimum. This is particularly important in the early morning and later at night when you could be accused of disturbing the peace. Those who want the privilege of having a dog park must be prepared to be fully responsible in every possible way.

To avoid fights, don't bring food or other edible treats into the dog park. There's no sense tempting fate. In these days when positive training has proven to be more effective than the old aversive methods, there are still, sadly, some people who are using choke, prong, pinch, or spike collars. Additionally, some people may not realize that dogs and puppies have been injured while playing with a dog who was wearing such a collar. Dogs should be wearing a flat buckle collar with identification and rabies tags for safety's sake.

Small children and toddlers do not belong in the dog run. In fact, children younger than twelve years of age can be problematic. Children should never be allowed to chase the dogs or run with them in the dog run. Children are loud and make sudden movements that could be startling to the dogs. These are not behaviors that many dogs understand if they're not accustomed to children. This is a play area for dogs only—not human children.

You can visit websites devoted to dog parks that will help you find one in your area. However, the responsibility is yours to decide if the individual dog park is safe enough for your dog(s) and to supervise your dog(s) while in the dog park.

DOG-PLAY.COM

This website has a good description of what constitutes a dog park and how to start one along with a wide variety of other activities you can do with your dog. It also has a list of dog parks.

For information: dog-play.com/dogpark.html.

THE DOG PARK.COM

This website is geared specifically to dog parks and has information on starting one, finding one, and more. While they have a training section, it uses an older methodology.

For information: thedogpark.com.

PUPPY PLAYGROUND

Children go to a playground, so why not puppies? And why not have playground equipment for your puppy in your own backyard? Either is possible. Puppy Playground locations can be found throughout the United States and you can take your dogs there for fun and socialization. They feature Puppy Playground equipment, which you can also purchase for your own backyard. Play nice and have fun are just two of the rules since safety is as important as having fun.

For information: puppyplayground.com; e-mail: info@puppyplay ground.com; telephone (toll-free): 888-828-3416 or (local): 904-673-8041; Puppy Playground, 1211 Golf Ave., Ormond Beach, FL 32174.

8

Off-Beat

Just when you think you've seen it all, something really fascinating comes along that you might not have known about. That's what you'll find in this chapter. Fun, different sights or activities that you might like to experience with, or without, your dog. But one thing is certain: it will be dog-related.

TRIBUTES TO FAMOUS DOGS

BALTO THE WONDER DOG

Gracing New York's Central Park is a statue to this glorious, heroic canine and the spirit of all sled dogs. During the 1925 diphtheria epidemic in Nome, Alaska, the town's only doctor put out a radio request urgently asking for antitoxin serum so that he could save the lives of those affected by the horrible disease. The hospital in Anchorage had it but the only way to get it to Nome in the middle of an Alaskan winter was via dog sled.

Balto was Gunnar Kaasen's lead dog for his team of Siberian Huskies. Following a handoff from the first team, Gunnar and his team brought the serum through the final, miserable fifty-three miles of treacherous travel. Blinded by the snow, Kaasen had to rely on Balto to find the way, which he did magnificently, and the epidemic was halted. The gallant Balto died in 1933 and was stuffed, mounted, and then put on display at the Cleveland Museum of Natural History. You can see him there today along with a film shot in 1925 showing Balto and the original team. The first diphtheria rescue team, however, was led by a dog named Togo. Togo is on display at the Iditarod Trail Sled Dog Race Gift Shop.

For information: Museum in Wasilla, off Mile 47, Parks Hwy., Wasilla, AK 99687.

JIM THE WONDER DOG MEMORIAL PARK

Yes, you read that correctly. This park in Marshall, Missouri, is named in honor of a Spaniel who died in 1937. Jim was a much-loved and well-known character in this midwestern town. When he was three years old, his owner realized that Jim acted as if he understood every word that was spoken to him. His responses were uncannily appropriate. Additionally, there are those who report that Jim could even make predictions.

Ultimately, after showing his abilities to respond to spoken requests to friends and neighbors, Jim and his owner were brought before a combined session of the State Legislature in Jefferson City in an effort to disprove the dog's ability. Needless to say, it was suspected that some sort of signal was involved between dog and owner. A test was created using Morse code, which Jim didn't understand. The test—which was an instruction telling Jim to walk to a certain person—was tapped out in the code; Jim passed the test and continued to select people from the crowd when asked to find someone with specific traits. He was unerring.

Jim is buried in Ridge Park Cemetery. He was originally buried outside the gate, but the cemetery expanded and includes his grave. His owners had no children and it was their wish to have him buried in a regular cemetery where people would visit his grave. The park was named in Jim's honor in 1999 and a statue of him was erected along with plaque stations throughout that each describe one of Jim's accomplishments.

For information: jimthewonderdog.com.

LAD, A DOG

Fans of Albert Payson Terhune who happen to be in Wayne, New Jersey, can visit the grave of his beloved first dog, a Collie named Lad, who died in 1918. Lad was commemorated in Terhune's children's book, *Lad, a Dog*, which has been beloved by readers for generations. Terhune was a Collie breeder who wrote children's books about his dogs, including other Lad books. He was a man of means who could do as he chose in life. Lad was buried on the Sunnybank Estate. Unfortunately, his marble slab marker and his grave rest in mud in what is now a park on Pompton Lake's western coast. The marker reads, Lad Thoroughbred in Body and Soul 1902–1918.

OLD DRUM

In a Warrensburg, Missouri, courtroom, then attorney and future senator George Graham Vest uttered these famous words to extol the virtues of Old Drum: "the one absolutely unselfish friend that a man can have in this selfish world is his dog." The dog, a hound, was shot and killed in 1870 by his owner's neighbor's nephew and ward. The neighbor was convinced that Drum had been killing his sheep. Charles Burden, who owned Drum, sued his neighbor. Ultimately, the case went to the Missouri Supreme Court, where Drum's owner won his case and the magnificent sum of fifty dollars.

Today you can visit a statue of Old Drum on the lawn of the Johnson County Courthouse. (The courthouse where Vest made his impassioned plea is elsewhere.) In a case of poetic justice, the man who shot and killed Old Drum subsequently moved to Oklahoma, where he was shot and killed.

OWNEY THE POSTAL MASCOT DOG

In 1888, a little mixed-breed dog was found abandoned outside the Albany, New York, post office. The employees brought him inside and put him into mailbags to keep him warm. He returned their care with the kind of love and loyalty that dogs give so unselfishly. Over the next ten years, Owney traveled, following postal workers over more than 140,000 miles, and he became known as "Globe-Trotter."

In 1897, Owney was shot and died. There is no record of who shot him or why. His body was stuffed and placed on display in a glass case. You can see Owney today at the National Postal Museum in Washington, D.C. It seems fitting that even after death he remains with the postal service.

For information: The National Postal Museum is at the corner of First St. and Massachusetts Ave. NE (next to Union Station), Washington, DC.

INTERNATIONAL

GREYFRIAR'S BOBBY

The little Skye Terrier, named Bobby, in Scotland who refused to leave his master's grave has gained prominence in the United States, thanks largely to a book written by Eleanor Atkinson in the 1890s. A life-size sculpture by William Brodie of the little dog is one of the most popular tourist attractions in Edinburgh. The sculpture is on a drinking fountain at Greyfriar's Churchyard. The dog was owned by a farmer named Jock Gray, who used to eat at an inn close to Greyfriar's Churchyard. When he died in 1858, little Bobby refused to leave his grave and he regularly appeared at the inn for fourteen years, where the locals would feed him because they were impressed by his devotion to his owner.

Whether or not the story has been embellished by the restaurant's owner is open to speculation. Another version of the story is that he belonged to a policeman. The dog was often in the churchyard and was cared for by people living in Candlemaker's Row, which is close to the cemetery. Greyfriar's Bobby died January 14, 1872, and his story was made into a film starring Donald Crisp in 1961.

For information: The statue of Greyfriar's Bobby is at the sharp junction of George IV Bridge and Candlemaker's Row in Edinburgh, opposite the entrance to Greyfriar's Kirk.

HACHIKO

A trip to Tokyo would not be complete for a dog lover without a visit to the Shibuya Train Station to see the statue of Hachiko. Akita lovers are well aware of this dog's story, and a book and movie have told his wonderful tale. Hachiko is commonly known as the most faithful dog in Japan. Whelped in 1923, he traveled to Tokyo in 1924, where his beloved owner, Eisaburo Uyeno, was a professor at Imperial University. The dog was closely bonded to his owner and would walk with him to the Shibuya Train Station every morning when he left for work. The professor would return at the end of the day to find his dog waiting for him at the train station, tail wagging happily.

In 1925, the professor became very ill at work and never returned home. Sadly, he died when Hachiko was less than two years old. The dog waited patiently at the train station every day, looking for his master to return. Sometimes the dog stayed away for days at a time.

Commuters became accustomed to seeing the dog, who was at the train station every day for ten years awaiting his owner's return. On March 8, 1935, Hachiko died. It is hoped that he and his owner were finally reunited. In 1934, artist Ando Teru was commissioned to sculpt a statue of Hachiko. It was the commuters themselves who arranged it because they were so affected by Hachiko's story and his faithfulness.

Unfortunately, the original bronze sculpture was melted down during World War II, but after the war, the Society for Recreating the Hachiko Statue commissioned the son of the original sculptor to create another bronze of Hachiko, which stands today at the same train station where this wonderfully loyal dog waited every day, all those years, for his beloved owner.

Each year on April 8th, a memorial service is held that attracts hundreds of dog lovers to the Shibuya Train Station to honor Hachiko's memory. Hachiko's body has been preserved and can be seen on display at the National Science Museum in Tokyo.

For information: kahaku.go.jp. (You can click on an English version.)

RIN TIN TIN ROADSIDE PET CEMETERY

While pet cemeteries can be found across the United States, you will find the grave of the American canine movie star Rin Tin Tin in a suburb of Paris called Asnieres. Near the Seine, the cemetery is actually called The Cimetiere des Chiens (et Autres Animaux Exotiques). His headstone is made of black onyx and has a gold leaf inscription.

Because the original Rin Tin Tin was actually found in the French trenches during World War I (others subsequently played Rin Tin Tin), it is somehow appropriate that he be buried in the country of his birth. The cemetery gets very few visitors and few dogs are now buried there, which makes it a candidate for extinction. As a result, it has been suggested that the dog's remains be moved to the United States.

TOURIST ATTRACTIONS

AKC MUSEUM OF THE DOG

Originally begun in New York, the AKC Museum of the Dog quickly outgrew its space at the AKC headquarters. It was relocated to a separate 14,000-square-foot building, which includes the historic Jarville House (1853) set in Queeny Park, in West St. Louis, Missouri.

Housing a wonderful array of dog art and memorabilia (with more in storage), in the past the museum has toured part of their collection, allowing it to be shown in other museums. The more than five hundred original works of art include decorative art, a Landseer oil on canvas of a Deerhound and recumbent Foxhound, and many of Maud Earl's portraits. On Saturday afternoons from February to mid-November, they feature an educational program and guest dog of the week.

There is a lovely gift shop on the property with items for you and your dog. The museum also has a book and video library (available by appointment), which can be used for research on purebred dogs and animal artists. An indoor and outdoor space is available for rental for meetings, dog-club activities, and special events.

For information: telephone: 314-821-3647; fax: 314-821-7381; The American Kennel Club Museum of the Dog, 1712 S. Mason Rd., St. Louis, MO 63131. (The museum is open year-round, Tuesday through

Saturday, 9 A.M. to 5 P.M., and Sundays, noon to 5 P.M. It is closed on Mondays and holidays.)

THE BIG DOG INFO CENTRE

Tirau, New Zealand, is the home to what is probably the most unusual information center in the world. Or, at least the one most in tune with dog lovers! The Centre is shaped like a dog and was built by Stephen Clothier of Tirau. It was the brainchild of John Drake, who owned the land the Centre was built upon and the Sheep—yes, there is another building in the shape of a sheep, which makes perfect sense since dogs are often used to herd sheep in New Zealand.

The Centre came about because the South Waikato District Council was searching for a place to put public toilets. The Council decided that the land belonging to Drake and his wife was perfect, but they didn't want to sell it for the sole purpose of placing public toilets there, and who can blame them! Drake and his wife suggested a sheep theme that could include a picnic area and parking lot. The Council wasn't interested but after the Drakes shared their idea with Henry Clothier, a local businessman, interest began to be aroused in the plan. Work began in January 1998 and the Centre was officially opened on September 25, 1998. Inside the Sheep you'll find a mural as well as a window painting, both scenes of the South Waikato area painted by local artists. The Centre is at the junction of three main highways and is only two hours south of Aukland. The Big Dog is open daily from 9 A.M. to 5 P.M. If you can't visit in person, you can see it online. *For information:* tirauinfo.co.nz.

CHICAGO WHITE SOX DOG DAY AFTERNOON

For dog owners who are baseball fans, the Chicago White Sox have an annual dog day. Fans are welcome to bring their dogs to a White Sox game at U.S. Cellular Field. On the dog day, fans are invited to enjoy the game side by side with their four-legged friends.

To make the day even more special, they will receive free health advice from veterinarians and visit dog-rescue organizations and animal massage therapists who are also at the ballpark that day. Additionally, dogs and their human companions have the opportunity to participate in a pregame parade. Dogs are admitted free of charge to a special section of the bleachers with the purchase of a game ticket. Advance reservation and proof of vaccination are required. Dogs must be at least six months old.

For information: whitesox.com; telephone: 312-674-1000; U.S. Cellular Field, 333 West 35th St., Chicago, IL 60616.

THE DOG COLLAR MUSEUM

Yes, there really is a museum devoted to dog collars. This historic collection of collars is housed at Leeds Castle in Maidstone, Kent, England. Leeds, reputedly one of the most beautiful castles, and the Dog Collar Museum are accessible to the handicapped, including a brochure in Braille that can be borrowed during the visit. There have always been dogs at Leeds Castle, from Mastiffs guarding the gates to Hounds kept for hunting, as well as Gundogs. And, of course, there were Lapdogs in the apartments of the widowed queens.

It's a true medieval castle surrounded by a moat, where black swans swim. The Dog Collar Museum is housed in the gatehouse, which had been a coach house and then a squash court. The collection was presented to the Castle Foundation by Mrs. Gertrude Hunt in memory of her husband, John Hunt. The collection has been increased and enhanced by the foundation.

Many of the collars go all the way back to the fifteenth century, and their spikes were designed to offer protection to the hunting dogs from attacks by wolves, bears, and wild boar. The collars from the seventeenth and eighteenth centuries are far more artistic in nature and are quite decorative.

For information: leeds-castle.com; e-mail: enquiries@leeds-castle.co.uk; telephone: +44 (0) 1622-765400; fax: +44 (0) 1622-735616.

FOUNTAIN OF WOOF

If you find yourself traveling the California coast, stop at the charming town of Carmel-by-the-Sea. Not only will you enjoy the art galleries and atmosphere, but your dog is going to want to move there. The Carmel area has a history of being dog friendly and dogs have always had the right to run free on the city's beautiful white-sand beach. Carmel Village Shopping Center has some shops that are supposedly pet friendly. It's wise, however, to ask if your dog is welcome.

Before World War II, Carmel adopted a dog named Pal, who is buried at Forest Theatre. You can still visit his grave marker.

Carmel has the very first official doggie drinking fountain in the United States, and, the whimsical fountain is in the shape of a life-size dog's head. The recirculating water spurts from the mouth onto a series of steps of rocky pools from which your dog can drink. It is appropriately named the Fountain of Woof and is located in Carmel Plaza. It was dedicated with a special event that included a canine fashion show and the reading of a poem.

For information: carmelplaza.com.

MOVIES IN THE PARK

Chicago is an extremely dog-friendly city. Dogs and their owners are welcome at Movies in the Park throughout the summer and early fall. You and your dog can see such family-oriented films as *The Wizard of Oz*, *Jurassic Park*, and the Harry Potter movies, among others. For a complete schedule of films being screened and locations go to the Chicago Park District website.

For information: chicagoparkdistrict.com.

STEPHEN HUNECK'S DOG CHAPEL

Yes, a dog chapel actually exists and is located in Vermont. Its motto is "Welcome All Creeds All Breeds, No Dogmas Allowed." Huneck, an internationally respected artist, is an avowed animal lover who shares his life with several dogs and a cat. The chapel contains a remembrance wall where visitors are welcome to place photos of their pets along with a message. Huneck built the chapel, following a near-death experience, to celebrate the bond people have with their dogs.

A Labrador Retriever with wings sits on top of the steeple to illustrate the special affinity with dogs. Inside you'll find dog carvings, stained-glass windows, and peaceful music to enhance the serene experience. A sculpture garden is in front of the chapel and the beautiful setting is enhanced by wildflowers that are planted on 7 of Huneck's 150 acres.

For information: huneck.com; telephone: 802-748-2700; Dog Mountain Gallery & Dog Chapel, Spaulding Rd., St. Johnsbury, VT 05819.

ST. HUBERT'S GIRALDA

Geraldine R. Dodge founded St. Hubert's Giralda in 1939 to serve animals and people by offering a wide variety of programs to nurture the human-animal bond. Mrs. Dodge was an ardent dog lover, famed breeder, exhibitor, and judge, and this is part of her legacy. It has served as a model for other organizations across the United States.

Among other services, St. Hubert's is an animal-welfare society. They also run a doggie day camp in the summer, and they offer a Paws for People therapy-dog program. Every October there's a Howl-O-Ween Hike. Their Tender Loving Critter Care program provides foster care—at no cost—for pets whose owners are in an emergency situation (such as a woman leaving an abusive spouse) until the individual is in a new home and can once again care for his or her companion. They also maintain a seven-day-a-week, twenty-four-hour-a-day, pet poison hotline. The call is toll-free, but there is a $35 incident charge for the service.

For information: sthuberts.org; e-mail: info@sthuberts.org; telephone (administrative): 973-377-7094 or (animal shelter): 973-377-2295; St. Hubert's Animal Welfare Center, 575 Woodland Ave., Madison, NJ 07940.

INTERNATIONAL

THE RED LION

This dog-friendly pub can be found in Baydon, Wiltshire, England. The owners, Alan and Jan Cole, have a Polish Lowland Sheepdog named Sophie, and they are kind enough to welcome all dogs and their owners to The Red Lion. It is close to the Ridgeway, and they promise that there are lots of lovely walks in the area that they'll be happy to tell you about. You can have bar snacks at The Red Lion or dine in their restaurant.

For information: telephone and fax: 01672 540348; The Red Lion, Ermin St., Baydon, Nr. Aldbourne, Wiltshire, 5N8 2JP, United Kingdom.

FUN WEBSITES

DOG HOROSCOPES

This amusing website will allow you to check your dog's weekly horoscope and see how compatible you and your dog are by comparing your zodiac signs. Click on Sirloin Tips, and below the humorous introduction you'll see serious bits of advice for dog owners. They also feature a Mystic Dog store where you can buy merchandise with their logo. Mystic Dog Newf (that's his name, not his breed) is the canine astrologer.

You can also post pictures and get a membership card and Mystic Dog decal by either e-mailing a photo of your dog in .jpg format or sending a photo by regular post. Be sure to include your dog's name, city or town, state, and country where you live, along with your dog's zodiac sign.

For information: doghoroscopes.com; e-mail: mysticdog@sprynet .com; Mystic Dog, P.O. Box 923, Farmington, CT 06034, USA.

THE PET DRIVER'S LICENSE®

In 1995, Chloe Cards postcard company opened, and in 1998 became the home of the Pet Driver's License. The full-color, laminated driver's license features your pet's photo on any state license and has the official Chloe seal. It's an amusing way to keep your pet's information with you at all times. The license is available as a wallet card, ID tag, key chain, carrier or luggage tag, digital file, or color wallet™ or can be transferred to a T-shirt or mouse pad.

And there's more, including Just Dig It™ T-shirts. Product descriptions can be found on the website. Once you've sent a photo, which will be returned, the image and information is kept on file and you can reference your order by your pet's name. You can order via e-mail, regular mail, or call toll-free. It's worth surfing over to the website just to read Chloe's amusing story.

Be sure to click on the link to learn why Chloe started the Pet Motor Vehicles (PMV). Every pet issued a Pet Driver's License at the PMV becomes an official member of DADD (Dogs Against Drunk Driving), of which Chloe is the founding member. You can get a license for any pet, even a stuffed one. It takes two to three weeks to receive the license. Chloe kits are available in some retail stores. You can find them listed at the website. Chloe Cards contributes to Best Friends Animal Sanctuary in Kanab, Utah.

For information: chloecards.com or petdriverslicense.com; e-mail: chloecards@aol.com; telephone (toll-free): 888-245-6388 or (local): 303-442-7790; Chloe Cards, 1118 13th St., Dept. 25-B, Boulder, CO 80302.

SHEEP GAME

If you've always wondered what it might be like to participate in a herding trial (or if you're looking for something to do while your dog is napping), this online, interactive herding trial is a fun way to pretend you're doing exactly that. There's actually more than one sheep game you can play, and the newest version allows you to build your own herding course. You will also find a downloadable version, one you can send to your own website, plus sheep-game wallpaper for your computer.

For information: david-lewis.com/sheepgame. You can also click over to the sister site, The Dog Game (doggame.co.uk).

VIRTUAL DOG SHOW

The Virtual Dog Show was created by Liz and Kynn Bartlett of Idyll Mountain Internet. It began in the fall of 1995 and has captured the fancy of dog lovers who surf the Internet. The event is run like a real dog show and is open to anyone who wants to have some online fun. All of the usual elements of a dog show are here from the entry form and an entry fee to the schedule, catalog, judges, prizes, sponsors, and vendors. Classes include brace, breeder, and junior classes and there are breed, group, and best in show winners chosen.

The site has a guide to how the show comes together. As the entries come in, the catalog is compiled online, and you can see the dogs. After judging is complete, you can surf back to see the winners. The judging panel consists of volunteers, many of whom have judged previous virtual shows and some are well-known dog show judges (yes, real shows), and from various Internet canine forums. Photos of dogs entered can be submitted in several ways so that even people who don't own a scanner can enter. Details are online, as are the details of how the judging happens. Dogs are, of course, judged strictly on looks since there's no way in which the judges can physically examine the dogs as they would at a real dog show. The virtual dog show is strictly for fun. *For information:* dogshow.com; e-mail: vds-admin@dogshow.com; telephone: 714-526-5656; fax: 714-526-4972; Idyll Mountain Internet, Liz and Kynn Bartlett, Owners, 110 East Wilshire Ave., Suite G-1, Fullerton, CA 92832.

EXPOS

GROOM EXPO

Groom Expo is a remarkable event, taking place in Pennsylvania each September. It is geared to anyone who makes a full- or part-time living from pet care, which includes grooming, training, boarding, day care, animal behavior, and pet sitting. The expo is also of interest to anyone who is a student or apprentice and wants to get seriously involved in professional pet care. Dog-show people can benefit from the expo's seminars.

For information: groomexpo.com or barkleigh.com; e-mail: info@bark leigh.com; telephone: 717-691-3388; fax: 717-691-3381; Barkleigh Productions, Inc., 6 State Rd. #113, Mechanicsburg, PA 17050.

OFF-LEAD TRAINING EXPO

The same people who present Groom Expo also publish *Off-Lead* magazine and present a training expo in California each winter and another in Pennsylvania in the spring. While they also offer grooming seminars, the main emphasis of the training expo is on dog sports as well as natural health for pets. It is open to anyone who has a particular interest in dog sports and/or training. The training expo is especially designed for individuals who make a full- or part-time living in training but it isn't exclusive to that. The education offered is geared toward someone who is teaching others or getting an advanced education. A new Natural Pet Expo is another annual event for all serious or professional people.

For information: barkleigh.com; e-mail: info@barkleigh.com; telephone: 717-691-3388; fax: 717-691-3381; Barkleigh Productions, Inc., 6 State Rd. #113, Mechanicsburg, PA 17050.

RADIO

These days you can go online and find radio networks devoted to animal-related programming. Some of the networks can be heard on various radio stations, which you can find listed at their individual websites.

ANIMAL PLANET RADIO

Animal Planet features a radio network that airs an hour-long weekly program hosted by pet journalist and broadcaster Steve Dale. Dale is colloquially known as the "pet guy." You can find his latest columns (changing weekly) and interviews online where you can hear his radio program. His guests include everyone from celebrities who are pet lovers and involved in various pet issues, to humane educators, veterinarians, authors, and more. Steve also has an online question-and-answer section at the website where he will answer your questions about pet health, behavior, and more. Programs are kept archived, so you can listen to what you might have missed. You can also view studio pictures and more.

For information: animal.discovery.com/fansites/radio/radio.html.

ANIMAL RADIO NETWORK

Animal Radio Network—which is part of Best Friends Animal Society—has a variety of broadcasts and airs on more than seventy radio station affiliates around the United States as well as on their website, where you can find a list of affiliated radio stations and various show hosts. They have also taken a mobile broadcast studio around the United States on what was billed as the Alfa-Dog Tour to find new homes for rescue animals. Various experts joined the tour at each stop as guests on each week's program. Joining the tour were four rescue cats adopted by the program's producers. Animal Radio™ is a not-for-profit organization; the experts and celebrities donate their time to the program. The programming on Animal Radio Network is geared to educating pet owners and all network advertising profits on Animal Radio directly benefit homeless, neglected, or abused animals.

For information: animalradio.com; e-mail: postmaster@animal radio.com; telephone: 805-236-0804; Animal Radio, 105 Meade Ln., Englewood, CO 80113.

PETRADIO.COM

PetRadio.com calls itself "The place where people and their pets sit, stay, and listen." The Internet radio station includes shows that feature animal experts; authors; representatives from humane organizations; creators of innovative pet products, books, and music; and more with topics ranging from flea control to legal issues. The shows fall into a range of categories listed on their website including news and talk, public service, and just for kids. PetRadio.com is a division of Shangri-paw Technologies and is a sister site of the Pet Project. Their Internet site links to Pets 911, which is a real-time, lost-and-found network to help people and their lost pets reunite.

For information: petradio.com; e-mail: info@petradio.com.

TELEVISION

Animal Planet, the U.S. cable television network, has programs that appeal to dog lovers. The following one invites you to audition with your dog to possibly appear on the show.

"PET STAR"

Do you think your dog is a star? Does he do special tricks or have some unique ability besides being a great companion? Can he dance or select specific coins for you? Do amazing stunts with a Frisbee? These are some of the tricks performed by dogs on the Animal Planet cable television network's show "Pet Star."

The one-hour show airs weekly, and it's not just a showcase for your companion; it's also a competition with cash prizes. Each week's winner receives $2,500 and is invited to return to be part of a final competition. One final winner will receive $25,000 in cash and prizes. He won't just be competing against other dogs but animals of other species as well.

The show is taped in front of a studio audience, and the contestants are initially judged by a panel of three celebrity judges. The highest-scoring pets are brought back at the end of the show, and the audience picks the winner. Auditions are held around the United States with announcements of upcoming auditions at "Pet Star"'s website. Alternately, you can send a VHS tape of your companion performing his best trick to the address that follows. For more information about upcoming auditions or VHS submissions, you can call the "Pet Star" hotline. The program currently airs every Friday night at 8 P.M. EST. Check your local listings.

For information: http://animal.discovery.com/convergence/petstar/ getonshow; telephone: 323-463-5040; "Pet Star," P.O. Box 2900, Toluca Lake, CA 91610.

"PLANET'S FUNNIEST ANIMALS"

This television program consists of a series of funny video clips provided by viewers, that feature their pets. The program provides humorous voice-over narration and viewers are invited to send their funniest tape in, which might be chosen to air on the show. If the producers use your tape, they will send you $100 and a "Planet's Funniest Animals" T-shirt. When you send in your tape, be sure to enclose a $3.50 handling fee if you want it returned.

For information: "Planet's Funniest Animals," P.O. Box 2904, Toluca Lake, CA 91610-0904.

INTERNATIONAL

"DOGS WITH JOBS"

On this program, dogs from around the world are shown working at a variety of jobs, including some that involve saving human lives, are high risk for the dog, or other jobs that they take on out of pure love. The jobs run the gamut from assisting the disabled to detecting land mines. You can watch video clips from the program on the show's website, which also features behind-the-scenes information on the dogs and their work. You'll also find a link to shop for things such as a video that features highlights from the show. Other links at the site will take you to sections on dog health, training, breeds, types of jobs dogs can do, dog quizzes, contests, and more.

For information: dogswithjobs.com; Cineflix Productions, Inc., Producer of "Dogs with Jobs" TV Series, 5505 St. Laurent Blvd., Suite 3008, Montreal, QC H2T 1S6, Canada.

FUND-RAISING DOG WALKS

One of the really wonderful, and fun, things you can do with your dog is join a fund-raising walk for animals to benefit a local humane society. While you and your dog are enjoying yourselves and the company of other dogs and their owners, you'll have the satisfaction of knowing that you're helping less fortunate dogs (and cats). Nearly every country seems to have them. Here are just a few:

ANIMAL FAIR MAGAZINE'S ANNUAL PAWS FOR STYLE

This gala springtime Manhattan event to benefit the Humane Society of New York is usually $100 per ticket. Limited tickets are available for the special evening. The highlight of the evening is canine couture, featuring a doggie fashion show with New York dogs strutting their stuff with their well-known owners. Of course, *Animal Fair* magazine's own Wendy Diamond and her little dog, Lucky, are among the glitzy New Yorkers participating in this event to benefit a worthy cause. The evening event includes cocktails and hors d'oeuvres, and there is a silent auction. And, in case you're wondering what to wear, dress calls for "canine chic."

For information: animalfair.com/events/paw; e-mail: events@animal fair.com; Animal Fair Media, Inc., 545 Eighth Ave., New York, NY 10018.

ATHENS RUN/WALK/ROLL

Sandy Creek Park in Athens, Georgia, is the site of the Athens Run/ Walk/Roll to benefit Canine Companions for Independence (CCI). The nonprofit organization provides highly trained assistance dogs at no charge to persons with disabilities and professional caregivers. Run/ Walk/Roll is for people and their dogs. Dogs must be on a leash. The human pays an entry fee, their dog gets in free. If you are among the first four hundred participants to register, you'll receive a T-shirt and a bandanna for your dog. The walks/runs vary in length and the roll is for people in wheelchairs. You can participate with or without a dog. There may be additional fees for some of the other events at this fund-raiser. There's Canine Good Citizen (CGC) testing, Therapy Dogs International (TDI) testing, and there's an assortment of dog contests including best bark, best costume (you can bring one for your dog to don for this event), best dancer, best dog/owner look-alike, best trick, fastest recall, smallest dog, and tallest dog. There are demonstrations, including canine musical freestyle, and there's a pet photo opportunity. Bring a picnic lunch and plan to have fun!

For information: http://ccirun.home.att.net.

BARK IN THE PARK

This fund-raising event to benefit the Progressive Animal Welfare Society (PAWS) in Lynnwood, Washington, is billed as a festival for dogs and the people who love them. PAWS, which is a nonprofit organization, was founded in 1967 and advocates for animals through education, legislation, and direct care. They are world renowned for their wildlife rehabilitation. Their companion animal shelter places approximately 4,500 to 5,000 animals in new loving, responsible homes each year.

The annual event takes place at Seattle's Sand Point Magnuson Park and features more than one hundred animal-friendly booths and vendors offering products, information, and food for both humans and animals. The event features photographers, doggie spas, animal products, and crafts. You and your pet can participate in doggie activities, contests, and demonstrations of clicker training, TTouch, search and rescue, and more, as well as attend informative lectures. There's music to enjoy and an off-leash area where your dog can play. Every pre-registered walker receives a T-shirt, a bandanna for his or her dog, and there are prizes for canines and their humans. You'll also meet dogs available for adoption. Bark in the Park begins at 9 A.M.; the PAWSwalk—to raise funds for PAWS—starts at 11 A.M. You can learn more about the walk at the Bark in the Park website, where you can also register, or your can call them directly.

For information: barkinthepark.com or paws.org; e-mail: info@paws .org; telephone (Bark in the Park): 425-742-4009; PAWS, P.O. Box 1037, Lynnwood, WA 98046 or (shelter address): PAWS, 15305 44th Ave. W, Lynnwood, WA 98046.

BARKUS AND MEOUX MARDI GRAS

If you're in New Orleans during Mardi Gras, you and your dog can participate in the Barkus and Meoux Mardi Gras, marching together to raise money for needy animals. The people who run the event divide the funds among several organizations dedicated to helping homeless animals, from shelters to rescue organizations. To qualify, they must be 501[c]3 charities and depend upon donations.

To participate in the parade, your dog must be up to date on vaccinations, on leash, and females cannot be in season. But everyone is certainly expected to be in costume as is appropriate for Mardi Gras. The event is run by Barkus, a nonprofit organization, and goes through the French Quarter. The royal court is introduced at the stage before the start of the lineup and royalty leads the parade.

The Mystic Krewe of Barkus was begun in 1992 at a local TV weather forecaster's fan-club meeting. Someone brought his dog to the meeting, and when people complained about the dog, the owner opted to make the dog the queen of her own parade and captain for life. Another dog was elected King Barkus I.

Each year the parade has a theme. Previous years' themes include "Welcome to the Flea Market," "Jurassic Bark," "Lifestyles of the Bitch and Famous," "Joan of Bark," and more recently, "Tail-House Rock: From Graceland to Jazzland."

Barkus merchandise is for sale at the website or at the event, where vendors are set up. You do need to pay an entry fee, which will increase as the date of the event gets closer.

Each registered Krewe member includes one human escort. Guests can walk with a Krewe member by purchasing an escort pass. To enter, you can fax your completed registration form, including a credit card number; you can mail it; or you can have it processed online at the Barkus website.

For information: barkus.org; e-mail: info@barkus.org; telephone: 504-581-BARK; fax: 504-522-0239; Barkus, 1000 Bourbon St., Suite 317, New Orleans, LA 70116.

DOG-A-THON

The Humane Society for Tacoma and Pierce County in Tacoma, Washington, holds an annual Dog-a-Thon the third Saturday in July from 8 A.M. to 1 P.M. It's held at Fort Steilacoom Park, which is an expansive and beautiful area in Lakewood. The event is emceed by local television anchors or "mild" celebrities.

To avoid having a large number of people and dogs on the trails at the same time, participants can walk whenever they choose, which makes it easier on the dogs. The humans have the option of arriving and walking whenever they choose during those hours. Walkers can choose from a one-mile stroll on a paved and flat path around the lake, which is great for elderly dogs, puppies, strollers, and those in wheelchairs, or a four-mile trek through woods and meadows with beautiful scenery at the top. The routes are well supported with designated stops for water, food, dog treats, and even toys.

More than one thousand dogs and at least as many people attend each year. In 2003, they raised $103,000 in pledges alone, which benefited homeless animals at the Humane Society. Everyone is welcome to participate even if they don't raise pledges. It's usually not too hot, but they have children's swimming pools, hoses, and shade for the dogs.

The event also features entertainment, a dozen or so dog-related vendor booths, police dog demos, agility, Frisbee, and service dog demos. They also present pet contests, such as best bark, owner look-alike, smallest, and best trick. You can enjoy music or participate in giveaways and drawings for prizes. It's no wonder people return year after year.

For information: thehumanesociety.org/dat/dogathon; telephone: 253-383-2733; The Humane Society for Tacoma and Pierce County, 2608 Center St., Tacoma, WA 98406.

DOG WALK AND PET FAIR

The Montgomery County SPCA was established in 1973 and serves Maryland, Virginia, and Washington, D.C. They are the only no-kill shelter in the National Capital Region. The MCSPCA is run entirely by volunteers and funded solely by private donations and fund-raising activities. Each October, they hold an annual Dog Walk and Pet Fair.

The walk is a leisurely 1.5 miles through Potomac, Maryland, followed by the Pet Fair and lunch. Participants receive a T-shirt, doggie bandanna, and a doggie bag of treats. You can, of course, participate if you don't have a dog. The walk begins at the Potomac Elementary School. There's an entry fee for each person who walks, with a reduced fee for children ages six to sixteen (children younger than six walk free). The fee is higher if you register on the day of the walk.

Check in for the walk between 9:30 and 10 A.M. The walk begins at 10:30 A.M., rain or shine. Dogs must have leashes and ID tags. Retractable leashes are not allowed, nor are vicious dogs, pups younger than six months old, or females in heat. Veterinary and medical aid are available in case of an emergency.

The Pet Fair that follows at 11:15 A.M. includes contests for best owner/pet look-alikes, owner/pet costume, best tail wagger, loudest bark, best newspaper retriever, and best dog trick. And there's a silent auction with wonderful prizes. To qualify for prizes, sponsorship money must be turned in before the walk. You can register for the walk online.

For information: mcspca.org; telephone: 301-948-4266; Montgomery County SPCA, P.O. Box 637, Washington Grove, MD 20880. Shelter location (do not send mail to this address): 402 East Diamond Avenue, Gaithersburg, MD 20880.

IT'S A DOG'S LIFE!

This two-day event in September, sponsored by Canine Sports Center in Goshen, Connecticut, is billed as a canine fund-raising extravaganza. You can bring your dog or find one to adopt at this event. Among the activities is a parade of rescues. These are the dogs who have found new homes where they'll always be loved family members. They also have a breed match; tattoo clinic; a pet photographer; agility and obedience run-throughs; "try its" in agility, freestyle, and flyball; a junior showmanship competition; canine good citizen testing; Frisbee dog demonstrations; search-and-rescue demonstrations; sledding and carting demonstrations; field, retrieval, and tracking demonstrations; and canine musical freestyle demonstrations. And, canine rescue organizations are there to tell you all about their dogs.

Prices for events are kept low, but preregistration is required for most events. And donations are very much appreciated. If the weather is inclement, some events are moved indoors. They also have fun contests like drooliest dog, best costume, most consecutive treats caught, "Lassie says," and more. All dogs must be on leash. The contest entries are only $1 each.

For information: caninesportscenter.com; telephone: 860-491-3904; fax: 860-491-3906; Canine Sports Center, 416 Old Middle St., Goshen, CT 06766.

JOAN THOMAS MEMORIAL WALK FOR THE ANIMALS

The first Saturday in October marks the Luzerne County SPCA's annual fund-raising walk, with all proceeds going to this humane organization. They accept any and all unwanted animals into their shelter and don't charge for the service. Pennsylvania has no state, local, or federal funds set aside for their SPCA, so funding must come from the community and events such as the annual walk. They keep all funds raised within the community to serve the local animals.

The walk takes place in Kirby Park in Wilkes Barre, Pennsylvania. Each walker must have a sponsor; in fact, the more the merrier because more money will go to the humane society. Dogs must be in condition to walk and must wear a suitable collar, which must be kept on the dog at all times. Dogs must be at least six months old, and you'll have to show proof of parvo, distemper, and rabies vaccinations. Your dog will also have to have a valid license from your county. No females in season will be allowed to walk.

Dogs are to be walked at a leisurely pace, and water is available for walkers and dogs at all checkpoints. If a dog or owner becomes tired, volunteers are on hand with cars and vans to take them back to the parking lot. Anyone who doesn't have a dog to walk can certainly bring a friend or neighbor—the more walkers at the event, the more money that is raised to help the animals. Walkers age twelve and younger must be accompanied by an adult. There is a ceremony at the end at which prizes are awarded. And there are commemorative T-shirts.

For information: dogsaver.org/spcaluz; telephone (shelter): 570-825-4111; Luzerne County SPCA, 524 E. Main St., Fox Hill Rd., Plains Twp., Wilkes Barre, PA 18702.

PAWS TO REMEMBER

The Long Island Alzheimer's Foundation (LIAF) holds an annual dog walk in September, called Paws to Remember. Funds raised help ensure that LIAF can continue to provide cutting-edge educational and social services to more than 135,000 Alzheimer's patients and their families throughout Nassau, Suffolk, Brooklyn, and Queens Counties.

The walk is a scenic stroll on a Gardiner County Park trail. Pet products on are display at the event, and you can have your picture taken with your family and your dog and join in other pet-related activities. A portion of the net proceeds are donated to Pet Peeves, a Long

Island nonprofit organization dedicated to benefiting abused, abandoned, and neglected Nassau and Suffolk County pets. They also collect bags and cans of pet food (cat and dog) on the day of the walk that will be donated to Pet Peeves, Inc.

There are fund-raising awards for walk participants, everything from tickets to a Broadway show to a pet grooming certificate. The walk takes place rain or shine. Dogs must be on leash or contained at all times, so you'll probably want to bring a crate or carrier with you so your dog can rest in the comfort of his own personal place. Dogs are screened as they check in. Those that are seen as a threat to other participants or female dogs in heat will be turned away. No retractable leashes are allowed. Your dog must be wearing an ID tag and be up to date on all vaccinations. Trash receptacles and "dispose-a-scoops" will be available. You are, of course, expected to clean up after your dog. *For information:* liaf.org; e-mail: info@liaf.org; telephone: 866-789-LIAF; fax: 516-767-6864; Long Island Alzheimer's Foundation, 5 Channel Dr., Port Washington, NY 11050.

PET PARADE—A WALK FOR ANIMALS

The Atlanta Humane Society calls itself much more than a shelter and is a place filled with unconditional love. They have a charitable veterinary facility, they do community education, and they are also a shelter resource throughout the Southeast. The Atlanta Humane Society invites you to put your best paw forward and join them in the fall at Six Flags over Georgia for their annual pet parade. This is Atlanta's largest pledge walk for pets to help those who don't have people of their own. You can even walk in recognition of a favorite animal friend and a special badge will be provided for you to wear. While pets are welcome at the pet parade, they are not allowed inside the park itself, so you will not be able to take your dog on any of the amusement rides. But there's so much more for you to enjoy at this dog walk including free refreshments, on-site microchipping, and doggie sports demonstrations and games that include doggie musical chairs, doggie limbo, and bobbing for burgers. There's paw print tile making, a souvenir photo for a nominal fee, face painting, and more.

For information: atlhumane.org; telephone: 404-875-5331; The Atlanta Humane Society, 981 Howell Mill Rd. NW, Atlanta, GA 30318-5562. (Humane Society hours are Monday through Saturday, 10 A.M. to 5 P.M., and Sunday, 1 P.M. to 5 P.M. The business office is open Monday through Friday, 9 A.M. to 5 P.M., but closed on the weekend.)

SAVE THE ANIMALS FOUNDATION

Save the Animals Foundation (STAF) is based in Gloucester County, New Jersey, and is a nonprofit, volunteer group. They provide financial assistance for spay/neuter surgeries, find permanent homes for companion animals, and provide financial aid for medical care for needy animals, as well as offering humane education. Their annual walk—truly a "walk in the park"—each October helps to fund their work, and the person who generates the most pledges wins a prize. All walkers who gather at least one hundred pledges will receive a T-shirt; and there are drawings and prizes for other awards. They also offer prizes for those who find a pumpkin along the route. STAF partners with the Gloucester Animal Shelter, who brings shelter dogs to the walk so those who want to participate but don't have a dog will have a canine companion for the walk. This win-win situation gives the participating shelter dogs a wonderful day in the park, and a few of them have even gotten a permanent home afterward. Their website provides a plethora of information on animal welfare, events, and companion animal health.

For information: http://advance8.tripod.com/staf; telephone: 856-218-7006; Save the Animals Foundation, Inc., P.O. Box 5689, Deptford, NJ 08096-0689.

WAG 'N' WALK

This fund-raising walk in Washington State is also known as Whidbey Island's Big Doggie Do. The event is a combined effort of two local nonprofits: Whidbey Animals Improvement Foundation (WAIF), who runs the local shelter, and Free Exercise Time for Canines & Their Humans (FETCH), who established and maintains Whidbey Island's five off-leash parks.

The annual event, which occurs in September at one of the off-leash parks, features vendors with all sorts of dog-related items for you and your dog, information and activity booths, and demonstrations. One of their goals is to show what wonderful companions you can get at a shelter. Each dog who receives a minimum of $35 in pledges for the walk receives a custom-made bandanna and their human will get a chef's apron.

The parade route is followed at a leisurely pace so everyone can enjoy the walk. Banner carriers and strolling musicians add to the festivity. And usually a contest is held as well. Check the website for details each year. They also look for volunteers to help with the event. *For information:* wagnwalk.org; e-mail: wagnwalk@whidbey.net; telephone (receives messages): 360-321-4580.

WALK FOR THE ANIMALS

The Massachusetts Society for the Prevention of Cruelty to Animals (MSPCA) was founded in 1868 and is one of the United States' oldest and most effective humane organizations. They have a very popular annual fund-raising walk in Boston each year that also includes a variety of events including an amateur dog show; a contest in which essays are submitted in advance, on topics such as What My Little Guy [guinea pig, gerbil, rabbit, rat, and so forth] Means to Me; a feline photo contest; an a-maze-ing rat display; face painting; arts and crafts; and a variety of contests, including owner and dog look-alike, best (doggie) vocalist, waggiest tail, best ears, best trick, and much more.

Their website has links to the MSPCA's home page or you can visit the society's website for more information and links.
For information: walkfortheanimals.org or mspca.org; telephone: 617-522-7400; MSPCA Headquarters, 350 South Huntington Ave., Boston, MA 02130.

WALK FOR THE ANIMALS

The annual walk for the Monadnock Humane Society in New Hampshire raises money to benefit the more than two thousand animals that go through their doors each year. Hundreds of people and their dogs turn out for this fun event. Great food, live music, face painting, kids' prizes, K9 Cops, a Canine Agility Training Society demonstration, doggie dancing, a critter talent contest, an amateur mutt show, a junior mutt show, and a feline photo contest all help add to the day's festivities. There are entry fees for the feline photo contest, the mutt shows, and the talent contest.

Check-in is at the Humane Society Adoption & Learning Center on Route 10, one mile south of Keene in West Swanzey. The walk begins in the afternoon, but festivities start at 10 A.M. and last until 2 P.M. You can pledge without walking, of course, but it's so much more fun to go and share the experience with your dog. Walkers who check in with $50 or more in contributions receive prizes and free admission to the Canine Carnival. If you raise $50, you receive a walk T-shirt, and there are some really fantastic prizes for the walkers who raise the most money. Past prizes include a week's vacation on Cape Cod, six months of free pet food, theater tickets, and more.

The walk takes place rain or shine. All dogs must be leashed, licensed, and up to date on vaccinations. Bring your dog's crate to the shady spot for rest periods during the day. Your dog should be wearing a buckle collar or Gentle Leader—no choke or prong collars. They also request that you not feed your dog before the carnival because he or she will be eating treats all day!

For information: monadnockhumanesociety.org; e-mail: monadpets@ humanecommunity.org; telephone: 603-352-9011 or (the walk pledge line): 603-352-0035, extension 207; Monadnock Humane Society, Route 10, P.O. Box 678, W. Swanzey, NH 03469.

WALK FOR THE ANIMALS—NANTUCKET, MASSACHUSETTS

The Massachusetts Society for the Prevention of Cruelty to Animals (MSPCA) has a wonderful facility on Nantucket and they have their own fund-raising walk. The mid-June event has changed each year to become more and more lively and interesting for the participants. It takes place at Children's Beach Park, a beautiful grassy area that overlooks the harbor.

Registration is in late morning, which gives people an opportunity to browse the booths that are set up that feature everything from pet food, Greyhound rescue information, marine mammal stranding team information, a cat center, pet supplies, and an MSPCA table selling hats, T-shirts, water bottles, and more. There's also a silent auction to bid on a variety of prizes. Dogs available for adoption wear "Adopt me" vests.

Once everyone is registered, the MSPCA mascots, Scoop and Scamp (a cat and dog respectively—well, people in elaborate costumes as a dog and cat), cut the ribbon to start the approximately two-mile-long walk that goes around downtown Nantucket.

Upon returning to the starting point, you can enjoy a picnic lunch, demonstrations such as agility, and activities such as face painting and tie-dying. You can purchase photo buttons that feature Scoop and Scamp and doggie pools are set up for the dogs to enjoy. Puppies available for adoption are in an x-pen. Prizes are given for "Mutt of the Year," "Fluff of the Year," "Most Money Collected," and "MVP" for the volunteer of the year. The silent auction prize giveaways are last but certainly not least.

For information: mspca.org; MSPCA/AHES, Nantucket Animal Hospital & Shelter, 21 Crooked Ln., Nantucket Island, MA 02554.

INTERNATIONAL

BCSPCA DOG WALKATHON

The British Columbia Society for the Prevention of Cruelty to Animals (BCSPCA), Sunshine Coast Branch, holds an annual fund-raising dog walk. As with other humane associations, they have an adoption program as well as one to foster animals before they find their permanent new home; they help reunite lost pets with their owners and they do humane education. Volunteers are the mainstay of this organization.

For information: spca.bc.ca/sunshinecoast; e-mail: sunshinecoast@ spca.bc.ca; telephone: 604-740-0301; shelter: 4376 Solar Rd. (off Field Road), Wilson Creek, BC V0N 3A1, Canada; shelter phone lines are open every day, 8 A.M. to 4:30 P.M.; donations are accepted at 4377

Solar Rd., Sechelt, BC V0N 3A1, Canada; they are closed Mondays and statutory holidays.

THE HIGH WYCOMBE DOG RESCUE ANNUAL SPONSORED DOG WALK

The Dog Rescue and Welfare Society in Stokenchurch, Buckinghamshire, England—which was founded in 1963 to save the lives of stray and police-impounded dogs—holds an annual sponsored dog walk. A registered charity, they also offer sanctuary to abandoned dogs from a wide area and their goal is to find a new, permanent home for each of them. To date, thousands have passed through this welfare society and have been placed in a new home. The walk begins at the kennel, which is situated on the A40 just west of Stokenchurch Village and within 250 yards of the M40 Junction 5.

For information: dog-rescue.co.uk/page3.html; e-mail: staff@dog-rescue.co.uk; telephone: 01494 482695; The Dog Rescue and Welfare Society, Tower Farm, Oxford Rd., Stokenchurch, Buckinghamshire, HP14 3PD, United Kingdom.

MILLION PAWS WALK

The Royal Society for the Prevention of Cruelty to Animals (RSPCA) in Australia holds a Million Paws Walk each May. Begun in Queensland in 1994, the event has flourished. This fund-raiser allows the RSPCA to continue its work in preventing animal cruelty, operating animal shelters, and providing animal welfare education in the communities. Major metropolitan walks take place in Melbourne, Sydney, Brisbane, Perth, Adelaide, Canberra, Hobart, and Darwin. In 2003, sixty walks were held around the country with more than 36,000 people and more than 26,000 animals participating.

The lengths of the walks vary, depending upon where they're held. Dogs must be on leash or otherwise restrained and must, of course, be healthy. During the walk, you can enjoy events in various venues, including stage entertainment, competitions, dog-obedience demonstrations, and shopping. You can also visit information displays or participate in veterinary checks or microchipping.

For information: millionpawswalk.com.au; RSPCA Australia, Inc., P.O. Box 265, Deakin West, ACT 2600, Australia.

WIGGLE WAGGLE WALKATHON

The Ottawa Humane Society has been in existence for more than 112 years and is a nonprofit organization. Their annual dog walk is their largest fund-raising activity and the money raised helps sponsor humane education, companion animal visitation, dog walking, adoptions, a foster care program, emergency animal protection services, and a lost and found service. The walk takes place each fall, and features other activities such as a barbecue, a kids' coloring contest, face painting, magic acts, dog grooming, a pet talent show, a dog agility demonstration, a dog wash, arts and crafts, doggie massage, nail clipping, goodie bags, and more. You can also visit a pet pavilion or purchase T-shirts. A smaller walk route is available for those who don't feel they or their dogs can do the longer route. Their website has some interesting information, including a useful links page.

For information: ottawahumane.ca; e-mail: ohs@ottawahumane.ca; telephone: 613-725-3166; fax: 613-725-5674; Ottawa Humane Society, 101 Champagne Ave. South, Ottawa, ON K1S 4P3, Canada.

NATIONAL EVENTS

AKC RESPONSIBLE DOG OWNERSHIP DAY

AKC Responsible Dog Ownership Day is an annual event that began in 2003. It was kicked off in Manhattan with an event in Central Park headed by Olympic Gold Medalist and dog fancier Greg Louganis, who brought along his Parson Russell Terrier, Nipper. Louganis spoke about all aspects of responsible dog ownership, including the importance of training, grooming, and exercise for companion dogs.

More than two hundred events took place around the country that same weekend to celebrate AKC Responsible Dog Ownership Day. It is expected that more dog clubs will participate each year. The events will be posted to the website beginning in July of each year and are listed by state. At least one international event (in Malaysia) occurred during the first year.

In Manhattan, dozens of children painted miniature DOGNY sculptures. The proceeds benefited the American Kennel Club's CAR Canine Support and Relief Fund, which assists search-and-rescue groups around the country.

The director of the AKC's Canine Good Citizen (CGC) program was at the event and conducted free tests. Events include pet adoption clinics; microchipping; CGC testing; and seminars on topics such as spay/neuter, health and nutrition, how dogs are trained to help the handicapped, programs for children, and more.

For information: http://akc.org/news/club_resp_ownership.cfm.

ANIMAL COMMUNICATORS

Physical and behavior problems are among the most common reasons people give for seeking out an animal communicator, while others do so when household changes are about to occur, such as a move or the addition of a baby to the family. The ability to communicate telepathically with an animal can yield accurate and helpful results under certain circumstances, such as if the dog is lost or sick. Often, the animal communicator can pick up on these feelings. This isn't witchcraft, but be on the lookout for charlatans. People who truly believe that they can communicate with animals are sensitive and propose that—although the dog may vocalize—communication occurs through visualization rather than specific words.

Here are some animal communicators:

LAUREN MCCALL

Lauren McCall is an animal communicator in Portland, Oregon. She explains that *animal communication telepathy*, *knowing*, *intuition*, and *empathy* are words that have been associated with animal communication. Her ability to communicate with animals exceeds the bounds of space—she can, and has, communicated with animals in other countries with striking results.

McCall encourages owners to set aside a little time each day to let their animals know just how much they mean to them. At The Integrated Animal, her office, you can take animal communication workshops.

McCall is a TTouch practitioner, level 2, and holds second- and fourth-degree Reiki. She has also studied with a number of animal communicators. McCall, a member of APDT, has worked and volunteered at animal shelters in the United States, Europe, and Southeast Asia. She does telephone consultations anywhere, as well as providing in-home services, if you live in the Portland area. Private consultations and workshops are available.

For information: http://integratedanimal.com; info@integrated animal.com; telephone: 503-704-7499; fax: 503-293-7298; The Integrated Animal, 8435 SW Carmel Ct., Portland, OR 97223.

KARLA MCCOY

Karla McCoy, who is in Peoria, Illinois, connects with animals telepathically through thoughts, pictures, words, and feelings. Her training includes basic and advanced animal communication courses taught by Carol Schultz and Amelia Kinkaid. She has helped people work through their concerns about their animal and has communicated with a variety of wild as well as domestic animals.

McCoy likes to have anywhere from six to eight questions prepared for the animal and while it's not necessary that she see a photo of the dog, it's helpful. She will ask the owner for the dog's name, age, breed, and a brief description. She also likes to have a brief history of any health or behavior issues or any current concerns the owner may have about the dog. This information helps her put her responses into context.

For information: e-mail: karlab@juno.com; telephone: 309-699-6935.

CAROL SCHULTZ

Carol Schultz's work with animals has included being a veterinary assistant with a local animal rehabilitation clinic. An animal communication specialist, Schultz wants people to better understand their companions' viewpoint, behavior, and needs. She begins with the premise that each animal is unique. She asks the owner to prepare his or her questions in advance and then asks if the owner has anything he or she would like to communicate to the companion animal.

Schultz teaches workshops in animal communication and you can find a schedule on her website. You can schedule a session with Carol Schultz either via e-mail or telephone.

For information: carolschultz.com; e-mail: carol@carolschultz.com; telephone: 815-254-8325; Carol Schultz, P.O. Box 509, Plainfield, IL 60544-0509.

PENELOPE SMITH

Penelope Smith is considered one of the pioneers in the field of animal communication. She has been an animal communicator for more than three decades and she uses the same counseling techniques that have helped people. Smith has both bachelor's and master's degrees in the social sciences, along with years of training and experience counseling humans, as well as in nutrition and holistic body energy balancing methods. She has also done research into animal anatomy, behavior, nutrition, and care. Smith has books and audio and video recordings available. And she conducts interspecies communication courses for those who would like to learn to communicate with animals. She can be consulted by appointment either in person or via telephone.

Smith will have a series of basic questions about the animal to facilitate communication and will ask that the owner have his or her own questions prepared. Her website contains a directory of animal communicators who subscribe to her code of ethics.

For information: animaltalk.net or (for German visitors): tierkommu nikation.de; e-mail: penelope@animaltalk.net; telephone: 415-663-1247; fax: 415-663-8260; Anima Mundi Incorporated, P.O. Box 1060, Point Reyes, CA 94956.

RUBBER STAMPING

Some wonderful dog stamps that can be used for a variety of purposes are available. For example, you can use a stamp of your dog's breed to decorate stationary. Or you can stamp a card for a special friend, create a cartoon "balloon" drawing coming from the dog's mouth, and add his special message to the card inside the balloon. Or you can use a paw-print stamp as your dog's "signature." Use a stamp to make bookmarks, gift enclosures, or decorate a special photo album. You're only limited by your imagination. Here are some companies that have dog stamps.

CATCH A FALLING STAR™

Catch a Falling Star has some wonderful dog-breed stamps. Some are holding a winner's ribbon in their mouth, others are holding an envelope, and some are just the dog with no embellishments. This is a home-based company, and the owners create the stamps themselves. Their website not only explains how the stamps are made, but also how to care for them so they'll last as long as possible. The stamps are for personal use and the owners post their copyright policy for use on the Web. You will also find a list of artists on their website.

For information: catchstar.com; e-mail (product and ordering questions): customerservice@catchstar.com or (company): imagine@catchstar.com; telephone (customer service for orders only): 516-541-8313 (Phone hours are Monday through Friday, 10 A.M. to 6 P.M., and Saturday, 10 A.M. to 3 P.M., EST.); fax (available twenty-four hours a day, seven days a week): 248-484-6210; Catch a Falling Star, P.O. Box 1149, Massapequa, NY 11758-1149.

INTERNATIONAL

ANDOVER RUBBER STAMPS

Andover Rubber Stamps are finely detailed stamps of all dog breeds. The company will even personalize the images with your name, address, and/or your kennel name. They also have paw stamps, ink pads, paper punches, and more including stamp cleaner. You can order online or by fax or telephone. They also have a large range of crystal giftware that can be personalized (engraved) for gifts or prizes with the same images that are on the rubber stamps along with any wording or message of your choice. The dog stamps are listed by group.

Among the fun and miscellaneous stamps are those depicting agility, obedience, and a bone stamp. They also have an address stamp on which you can have your name, address, and/or telephone number. You can purchase an address stamp with two dog-breed images of your choice. They also feature a bone stamp, to which you can add your name and address.

For information: dogrubberstamps/dogs; e-mail: service@andover rubberstamp.com; telephone: 01264 362925; fax: 01264 333709; Andover Rubber Stamp Service, Unit 1, Balksbury Estate, Upper Clatford, Andover, Hampshire SP11 7LW, United Kingdom.

Even though I've found so many dog-related items, websites, and adventures, I wouldn't be surprised to find more with each passing day. You will always find new ways to have fun with your dog, treat him to something special, or take better care of him. Dogs are our companions, friends, and often soul mates. We bring them into our homes to enhance our lives. We take care of them and they reward us with unconditional love. When we share more with them, the human-animal bond strengthens. How nice that there's so much to share! I wish you happy days filled with the love of your dogs. Now go out and have some fun!

Index